When News Was New

When News Was New

Terhi Rantanen

WILEY-BLACKWELL

A John Wiley & Sons, Ltd., Publication

This edition first published 2009
© 2009 Terhi Rantanen

Blackwell Publishing was acquired by John Wiley & Sons in February 2007. Blackwell's publishing program has been merged with Wiley's global Scientific, Technical, and Medical business to form Wiley-Blackwell.

Registered Office
John Wiley & Sons Ltd, The Atrium, Southern Gate, Chichester, West Sussex, PO19 8SQ, United Kingdom

Editorial Offices
350 Main Street, Malden, MA 02148–5020, USA
9600 Garsington Road, Oxford, OX4 2DQ, UK
The Atrium, Southern Gate, Chichester, West Sussex, PO19 8SQ, UK

For details of our global editorial offices, for customer services, and for information about how to apply for permission to reuse the copyright material in this book please see our website at www.wiley.com/wiley-blackwell.

The right of Terhi Rantanen to be identified as the author of this work has been asserted in accordance with the Copyright, Designs and Patents Act 1988.

Library of Congress Cataloging-in-Publication Data

Rantanen, Terhi.
  When news was new / Terhi Rantanen.
    p. cm.
  Includes bibliographical references and index.
  ISBN 978-1-4051-7552-4 (hardcover : alk. paper) — ISBN 978-1-4051-7551-7 (pbk. : alk. paper) 1. Journalism. 2. Broadcast journalism. I. Title.
  PN4731.R36 2009
  302.23—dc20

                                             2008054075

A catalogue record for this book is available from the British Library.

Set in 10.5 on 13 pt Minion by SNP Best-set Typesetter Ltd., Hong Kong
Printed and bound in Malaysia by Vivar Printing Sdn Bhd

01 2009

In memory of Roger Silverstone 1945–2006

Contents

Figures and Tables

Figures

Tables

Acknowledgments

My sincere thanks to Tamar Ashuri, Oliver Boyd-Barrett, David Brake, Matthew Collins, Richard Collins, John Entwisle, Gordon Gow, Annie Jackson, Jean Morris, Margot Morse, John Nerone, Eila Nieminen, Erik Nylén, Shani Orgad, Michael Palmer, Peter Putnis, Donald Read, Roger Silverstone, Elizabeth Swayze, Henrik Örnebring and Elizabeth Van Couvering for their help. My very special thanks to Jean Morris for revising my language and rescuing me from being lost in translation.

I am also grateful to the Annenberg Center for Communication at the University of Southern California, the British Academy, the European Alliance of Press Agencies, the History Section of the IAMCR and Reuters archive.

Terhi Rantanen
November 2008

Introduction

When News Was New

INTERVIEWER: Do you know what news is?
TIMO (six years old): It tells us what has happened in every country and then what the weather is going to be like.
INTERVIEWER: What kind of pictures do you see on TV news?
NIINA (six years old): Exciting.
INTERVIEWER: How are they exciting?
NIINA: Such as a fire or a burnt house.
INTERVIEWER: How do you feel when you see these pictures?
NIINA: I actually like them. I don't know why I like scary pictures and exciting stories. (Pennanen 2007, 17)

This book asks a simple child-like question: "What is news?" By asking this question it interrogates the individuals and institutions that make, manufacture, and produce news. It investigates how news has re-invented itself at different historical *moments* – from medieval storytellers, to nineteenth-century telegraph news agencies, to twenty-first-century bloggers. It is not a journalism history book that claims to cover all historical periods, but rather it chooses instances, moments when there has been a change. Neither is it a progressive history. By choosing present and past historical moments, it problematizes the concept of progress in news and finds unforeseen similarities between different moments. Finally, it asks whether news, as we think we know it, actually exists any more.

This book is about news in the past, the present, and the future. It argues that newness in news has regularly, over the centuries, been reconstructed and that news is mostly old stories made new. At the same time, these stories inhabit temporal and spatial structures that challenge our ideas about our mental space in the past, the present, and the future. Rather than asking whether news is "objective," the book explores the temporality and spatiality of news, in order to show how it changes not only itself but the space around it. This is a book that reaches out from journalism studies to see the wider social implications of news.

Too much has been written about the objectivity of news and too little about news as a cultural, economic, and social good whose temporal and spatial features keep changing. News is so widely recognized as news that it is not easy to understand its wider significance. We may look at what is inside news but what we see is what we have been taught to recognize. We may think news is just news, an ephemeral piece that informs us about the world. What we may not realize is that, by following the agreed conventions that makes it recognizable as news, it sets up a framework within which its predefined elements are related to each other. By concentrating on what news is about, what its content is, we ignore its structural elements. As a result, such important elements as time and place in news have been taken for granted and left unproblematized. I shall argue that a historical analysis of news is needed in order to understand how the understanding of the nature of news changes in space and time. Only by looking at the historical development of news can we understand when and how news became new.

Temporal aspects in news have been understood mechanically as "when," without any understanding of the social construction of time. There are many ways in which news can be made new. Between 1500 and 1800, hawkers and ballad-mongers performed *new stories* next to bear-wards, buffoons, clowns, comedians, and hocus-pocus men (Burke 1994, 94–95). New stories were often old and did not look like what we now know as news, but did have elements that would later come to be recognized as characteristics of news. Later, from the mid-nineteenth century, the mass production and frequent, regular mass distribution of news meant that news became an important marker of time. Gradually "no news" became an impossibility of the modern age.

But now, on the Internet, rather than marking time, news is on *all* the time. With the emergence of online news, new forms of new stories have emerged. In 1999 it was noted that dozens of blogs had appeared; there are now millions. As with the new stories of the Middle Ages, modern bloggers "sing" their stories, next to a variety of other performers, not on the street corner but on the node of the World Wide Web. Nothing "travels" any more: not news, nor its producers nor its consumers; they all meet virtually on the World Wide Web. The era of "pure" news is over: everybody who has access to technology can now be a singer of new stories.

The spatial aspects of news are often thought of as "where," without any understanding of the social construction of place or space. Not only does news travel lightly between places, but it also creates new spaces. News creates news spaces, whether these are within the boundaries of cities, of nation-states or of the World Wide Web. Navigation is provided inside news, and the users of news navigate in news spaces, creating new networks.

My book is not a conventional history and does not present a chronological history of news. Rather, it analyzes the social construction of news in a historical context. It theorizes the development of news, using examples from different historical periods. It argues that, by analyzing the temporal and spatial aspects of news, we understand why the definition of news has changed. What kind of news is needed in different historical moments is deeply influenced by the temporality and spatiality of news. It is only by exploring these structures in news that we can understand its social functions.

Chapter Outline

Chapter 1: Temporalization: How News Became New

That "news is new" appears as self-evident as that "a rose is a rose." The salience of time in news has resulted in the "naturalization" of its temporal aspects – we do not see how novelty is constructed in news. I argue that there are at least four ways in which news is made new. First, news may be presented as a new genre. Second, the "event" that news is about is constructed as new. Third, news is presented as new even if the "event" it is about is old, because a particular news audience did not previously know about it. The fourth aspect of temporality in news is its regularity, the impossibility of "no news," "no novelty, nothing new," that implies how news temporalizes societies, setting up news time, a new global time.

Chapter 2: Cosmopolitanization: An Older Phenomenon Than We Think

In this chapter I argue, in contrast to earlier research on the relationship between "national" and "international" news, that news was not originally "national" or "international," but cosmopolitan. News was mainly exchanged between cities. Introducing cities as a starting point for analysis opens up new ways of understanding empirical materials that have previously been theorized only in terms of the national–international framework. I explore the birth and development of news exchange in and between major cities in Europe from the twelfth until the nineteenth century, and how this changed with the advent of new communications technologies such as the printing press and the telegraph. I argue that the transmission of news is connected to territorial transformation, changing cities into cosmopolitan spaces that became world cities. This chapter is a revised version of an article already published in *Journalism Studies* 8(6) (2007), 843–861.

Chapter 3: Globalization: When News Became Global

This chapter contributes to the debate on the timing of globalization and the role of electronic news in globalization. I argue that news played a key role in globalization, via the early submarine cable networks, as early as the latter half of the nineteenth century. The manipulation of time and space on a global scale was an essential component in the commodification of news. This chapter argues that the new global news space was not frontierless but that, on the contrary, the news organizations, in pursuit of their commercial ends, erected a series of impermeable barriers which they controlled. This chapter is a revised version of an article already published in *Media, Culture and Society* 19(4) (1997), 605–620.

Chapter 4: Commodification: How To Sell News

Nineteenth-century electronic news was a new cultural good of its age, but differed from other information goods because it rapidly became an exclusive good from which not everybody could benefit. The telegraph revolutionized news transmission: it conveyed messages at the speed of electricity, whilst other goods could only be physically transported. This broke with established circulation patterns for news and information, which like other goods had formerly had to be physically transported. The creation of this new product gave birth to weightless goods, provided by global news organizations, anticipating a new global information society that came into being with the World Wide Web. The struggle over the nature of news – whether it is for particular groups or for everybody – continues.

Chapter 5: Localization: Places in News

In this chapter I analyze the early historical development of place in news. Most news studies either focus on the content of news (or the "event") or, if they pay attention to the geography of news, as in the news flow tradition, they focus on the nation-state from which the news originates. This chapter examines how a sense of place was constructed in electronic news from the Middle Ages to the mid-nineteenth century. I argue that electronic news increased the sense of place by organizing space, and its readers were able to distinguish between "there" (where news came from) and "here" (where home was). This chapter is a revised version of an article already published in *Media, Culture and Society* 25(4) (2003), 435–449.

Chapter 6: Nationalization: News and the Nation-states

I present three case studies on the development of "German," "Russian" and "US" agencies, each of these being very different politically and culturally, but, in the later nineteenth and early twentieth century, all arguing for the necessity for news to serve national interests. The history of news organizations shows how the first electronic media, the telegraph and the wireless, were constructed primarily in order to serve national interests. The independence of news organizations was vulnerable to state control of the telegraph and the wireless radio.

Chapter 7: Epilogue: Today Was Yesterday

This chapter argues that yesterday's news is also today's news. It examines the "new" news in the Information Age. It discusses news singers, news-gatherers and bloggers and the similarities and differences between them. It argues that "newness" has again been re-invented. What we are witnessing now is the death of "modern" news, as conceived in the nineteenth century. In this situation of multiple change, serious thought is required about what constitutes news.

1

Temporalization

How News Became New

"What news on the Rialto?"
   (*William Shakespeare*, The Merchant of Venice, *Act I, Scene III*)

What's the news? What's the latest news? Any news? No news? There is probably nothing as temporal as news. In most languages, the very word for news refers to its temporality: *news* in English, *nouvelles* in French, *novosti* in Russian, *uutinen* in Finnish, *nyhet* in Swedish all have "new" as their root word. The dictionary definition also includes temporality: "tidings; reports or accounts of *recent* (esp. important or interesting) *events* or occurrences, brought or coming to one as *new information*" (my emphasis). An early use of the word can be found in 1382 in the Bible (Wycliffite, E.V.): *Ecclus.* (Bodl. 959) xxiv. 35 "þe whiche fulfilleþ as phison wisdam & as tigris in þe daiys of newis."[1]

That "news is news is news" thus appears as to be as self-evident as that "a rose is a rose is a rose." As a result, unfortunately, the *temporality* of news has been neglected, or rather taken for granted, in academic research because it is considered too obvious. The salience of time in news has resulted in the "naturalization" of its temporal aspects. As a result, time is often understood in news only as mechanical time, rather than as socially constructed.

What is news in each historical period depends completely on how time is socially constructed in news. Journalism researchers have stated, for example, that there are three kinds of timeliness: first, there is recency (recent disclosure); second, there is immediacy (publication with minimal delay); and third, there is currency (relevance to present concerns) (Roschko 1976, 11). However, these categories are not fixed and change over time and space. Even if these categories clearly contribute to the breaking down of time, they still take time as "God-given," without problematization or understanding of the historical changes that have taken place in news.

In order to understand how the temporalization of news operates, we need to look at the definition of news. Just looking at the dictionary definition presented earlier, we see that news is supposed to consist of two elements: *recent events* and *new information*. This is a step in the right direction, identifying time as a component of news, but it remains unsatisfactory because it assumes a natural connection between events and time.

An alternative approach is to explore academic research that attempts to understand what news is. Gans (1979, 250) has divided into three different categories the theories about how certain stories are selected for the news: (1) journalist-centered; (2) the sheer habit of news organizations; and (3) event-centered. The third category approaches news as "a social construct, emphasizing the human agency involved in news, the informal rules which journalists adopt in order to process vast amounts of information and to select and repackage it in a form that audiences will accept as *The News*" (Gitlin 2003, 250). This approach also includes "the idea of news as a *narrative*, primarily a matter of fact, of data, of particulars which tell a *story*" (Shaaber 1929, 4).

According to Gitlin (2003, 250), the third category of theorization is event-centered because it argues that news "mirrors" or "reflects" the actual nature of the world. Again Gitlin's argument takes us in a direction different from mine. My primary interest is not in the mirroring or reflecting function of news, but in the ways it is constructed as a narrative that follows its own rules. Hence, for the purpose of this chapter, the "objectivity" of news is not the primary interest. Gans is helpful here, since he offers a synthesis of the three different approaches by defining news as "*information* which is transmitted from *sources* to audiences, with journalists [. . .] summarizing, refining and altering what comes to them from various sources in order to make the information suitable for the audience" (Gans 1979, 80, my emphasis).

However, the difference between news and information is not necessarily as unproblematic as this definition assumes. On the contrary, I would argue that it is the temporalization of news that has not been recognized as a key element in the distinction between "information" and "the news." For the purposes of this chapter, I define news as a specific type of writing that uses the *concept* of time and of an event in order to construct a new story. It is important to notice that every new story is not necessarily a news story and separating news from new stories by labeling it as "news" becomes of crucial importance.

Traditionally, in news studies, a distinction has been made between an event, a source and news (see for example, Galtung and Ruge, 1965). An event does take *place*, often far away from the news source and the people who are interested in it. The introduction of the concept of place into the understanding of the "newness" of news adds another dimension: the distance between the place of an event, of a source, and of the news. An event takes place, while travel takes *time*, and any change in distance, as well as the overcoming of distance, has an effect on the newness of news. The French word *jour*, the root word for journalist, journalism, and journal, is also a root word for journey. In its original meaning, a journey was a day's travel, which quickly became extended to also refer to something that could be measured by the specific number of days required (Harris 1978, 120). The word journalist came into use in 1693 to describe those who wrote about *daily* doings for the public press (Harris 1990, 172). Hence, the connection between news, event, travel, and time defined in terms of days was constructed at an early stage.

Important as it is to note that new stories travel over distance, they also travel over time. New stories travel from generation to generation through memory. In so doing they are transformed from old stories into new stories, since a story is news for those who have not heard it before.

In this chapter I explore the temporal structures linking an event, an item of information, a source, and an audience of new/s stories. I argue that new technology has changed the relationship between all these. The newness of news no longer implies merely a closeness between the source and the audience, but that events, information, source, and audience have almost become one. This is the situation in which the temporalization of news has fundamentally changed the structure of news as we have learned to recognize it.

New Stories and Memory

Darnton (2000, 1) writes that the nature of "what constitutes news" varies considerably between different societies. He cites examples from studies of coffee houses in Stuart England, tea houses in early Republican China, market places in contemporary Morocco, street poetry in seventeenth-century Rome, slave rebellions in nineteenth-century Brazil, runner networks in the Mogul Raj of India, even the bread and circuses of the

Roman Empire. However, in *oral* news, people had physically to be in the same place at the same time in order to be able to exchange new stories. When people gathered together in the market place or in the church square it was easier to distribute new stories from one to many or from many to many.

In preliterate cultures, information that was important or sacred was often transmitted to new generations in the *form* of a story, for example a narrative poem. Pentikäinen (1989, 84) writes

> Under these circumstances, poetic form served as a technical aid to memory, whereby *particular details came to be repeated* more precisely than in prose narratives. Living poetry which exists as oral tradition is not, of course, preserved as such, but is disposed to change, facilitated by various cultural and individual factors. A rune may be handed down from one generation to the next, but each generation treats it in accordance with its own conceptual world. (My emphasis)

A story could be told and memorized, but this was not necessarily a news story, even if was a new story. It had elements of structure which are found in news stories ("once upon a *time*"), but time and place were not necessarily the most crucial aspects of the story's structure. These were in a way timeless and placeless stories, since what mattered was not the time of the event, or even the place of the story, but that the story had not been heard before. Their newness was not in the story itself but in their audience who have not heard it before and needed to remember it. These stories had two distinctive features: they were based on memory and on repetition. Clanchy (1994, 3) writes of the Middle Ages:

> Outside the king's court and great monastic houses, property rights and all other knowledge of the past had traditionally and customarily been held in the living memory. When historical information was needed, local communities resorted not to books and characters but to the oral wisdom of their leaders and remembrancers.

In this way, the distinction between what was news and non-news was not always clear even in the Middle Ages. As Shaaber (1929, 189–190) observes, there was an old habit of making up songs about passing events, battles, feuds, raids, murders, and domestic tragedies and remembering these, perhaps even all around the world, in the form of popular ballads. According to Shaaber (1929, 190):

these ballads, steeped in repetition, [were] almost borne down by its refrain, plunging abruptly into a situation, describing no characters and often not naming them, telling no long story and easy of pace, free of repetitions, bare of refrain, abounding in details and covering considerable stretches of time.

As a result, new stories, in forms such as poetry or ballads, had a much longer life than news. They were memorized, repeated, and partly changed from one generation to next. The elements of regularity and repetition were already present in the *form* of new stories. They were often old stories, but became new by traveling through time and space, by changing place but simultaneously becoming placeless, spaceless, and timeless. There are several examples of how one particular story travels in time and space, gets translated, and pops up somewhere else as a new story (Shaaber 1929, 201). But oral new stories were about to change with the introduction of writing.

Written New Stories

Time was determined in agrarian communities by the rhythms of nature. Ong writes that before writing people did not feel themselves to be situated at every moment of their lives within any sort of abstract computed time. It appears unlikely that most people in medieval or even Renaissance Western Europe would ordinarily have been aware of the number of the current calendar year – whether this was dated from the birth of Christ or from any other point in the past (Ong 1982, 97–98). As Giddens (1990, 17–18) has pointed out, communities lived distinctively, following their own local times. "When" was almost universally connected with "where" or identified with other natural occurrences, and time was still connected with place. According to Gurevich (1972, 94), the peasant's calendar reflected the alternation of time, following the succession of the agricultural seasons. In many languages, the months still reflect the agricultural and other tasks of the respective months. For example, in Finnish, May is *toukokuu*, the month of sowing, June is *kesäkuu*, the month of summer, July is *heinakuu*, the month of haymaking, and August is *elokuu*, the month of harvesting.

There was no need for measured time. Until the thirteenth and fourteenth centuries, instruments for measuring time were rare objects of luxury. The most usual forms of clock in medieval Europe were the sundial, the sand-clock, or the clepsydra (water-clock) consisting of a candle or oil in a sanctuary-lamp (Gurevich 1972, 102, 105). If it was absolutely necessary to know the time at some point after sunset, this was measured by the burning down of a torch (Gurevich 1972, 105). According to Gurevich, the length of a journey was measured by the time spent at sea or on foot or horseback. It occurred to no one to imagine a journey between two points in terms of time measured in abstraction from the traveler making that journey. Time, in archaic society, was not something external to people, unrelated to their lives and doings (Gurevich 1972, 102–103). The same principle could be applied to new stories that included no mention of measured time.

Time, apart from agrarian time, was considered either not to matter or to be a matter for the Church. Le Goff (1980, 29–30) makes a distinction between the Church's time and a merchant's time in the Middle Ages. The church set up its own time which belonged to God alone and could not be an object of lucre. Monks reckoned by the number of pages of holy scripture they had read, or by the number of psalms they had sung between two observations of the sky. For the mass of the people, the main time signal was the sound of church bells, calling them regularly to morning prayers or other religious services. Thus when collective time became more important, the *recorded* passage of time would still be controlled by the clergy (Gurevich 1972, 105).

A significant change took place when writing was introduced. The memorization of stories lost its crucial importance, because these could now be stored by writing them down. Repetition within stories thus also became unnecessary, saving time and space. The shift from memory to written communication, which occurred in England in the twelfth and thirteenth centuries, was not restricted to England, although it is more evident there (Clanchy 1994, 5). This resulted in an early temporalization of recorded events: *chronicles*, a continuous historical account of events arranged in time order without analysis or interpretation. Clanchy observes that the typical chronicle was a cumulative memorial, was monastic, and had its origins in the Benedictine preoccupation with the careful regulation of time. He writes

> The typical chronicle was thus a *dated series of events* recorded for the guidance of a monastic house. The chronicler computes years *Anno Domini* and months and calends and briefly describes the actions of kings and princes

which occurred at those times; he also commemorates events, portents and wonders. The chronicle was thus an unstylish production, concerned with the matter rather than the manner of presentation, and added to year by year and therefore by various people. (Clanchy 1994, 100, my emphasis)

Clanchy also writes that a distinction could be made between memorable events (*memorabilia*) and those worth remembering (*memoranda*); only the latter, which are really worthy of memory, should be recorded. Far from advocating the mass-production of literature or documents, the monastic writers aimed to record for posterity a deliberately created and rigorously *selected version of events* (Clanchy 1994, 147, my emphasis). This division, of course, will have important consequences for the future concept of news that records only newsworthy events.

If one wanted to reach out of one's own place, one had to send a message or a letter. An oral message could be repeated word for word by the messenger, but a letter had to be written. Because of the wide gap between ordinary uneducated people and the cultivated elite, intellectual culture became the monopoly of the church (Le Goff 1980, 155). Writing and reading were thus restricted to the church and to the upper classes who could also write letters. These were hand-written and contained information about a particular event or series of events that their writer considered important and wanted to be delivered over distance.

Letters were combined with oral communication. Darnton (2000, 1) writes that in seventeenth-century Paris there were newsmongers (*nouvellistes de bouche*) who gathered under the Tree of Cracow which stood at the heart of Paris in the gardens of the Palais-Royal and spread information about current events by word of mouth.

> They claimed to know, from private sources (a letter, an indiscreet servant, a remark overheard). There were several other nerve centres for transmitting "public noises" (*bruits publics*), as the variety of news was known, especially benches in the Tuileries and Luxembourg Gardens, informal speakers. Corners on the Quai des Augustins and the Pont Neuf, cafés known for their loose talk, and boulevards where news bulletins were bawled by peddlers of *canards* [facetious broadsheets] or sung by hurdy-gurdy players. To tune into the news, you could simply stand in the street and cock your ear. (Darnton 2000, 1)

Letters started with a date and place, indicating the distanciation between the places they were sent from and those to which they were delivered. At the same time, hand-written letters recorded information and did not rely on memory. The space for writing was restricted by the size of the paper (Gurevich 1972, 104). Letters were mainly for collective, not only individual, use. They carried information that was new if the recipient did not know it. The expression of time was still problematic, even in letters. Monastic correspondence used an expression related to papal years or *Anno Domini* (in the year of the Lord). Non-religious documents found it difficult to specify a numerical year. Clanchy (1994, 302) writes that everybody knew which year was meant – the present one – and that if there was any doubt, some *notable event* could be referred to. He gives an example:

> The 1181st year AD, the 21st year of Pope Alexander III, the 27th regal year of King Henry II of the English, the 11th regal year of King Henry the son of the king, the 18th year that has passed since the translation of Bishop Gilbert Foliot from Hereford to London, when this inquest was made by Ralf de Diceto, Dean of London, in the first year of his Deanship. (Clanchy 1994, 303)

The Church established its own time marked by important events with the publication of calendars and almanacs. Later almanacs grew out of printed church calendars and always included a record of saints' days. To this were added astrological information and then the illustration of the labors of the months (Hönig 1998, 130). Pamphlets that concentrated on singular events were often called "relations," later "newsbooks" (Stephens 1988, 87).

As Stephens writes (1988, 54), news moves fast, but writing is slow. In the past, letters were delivered by messengers. They traveled exactly as fast as the messenger. Travel, especially on roads, was slow, tiresome, and even dangerous. In the early Middle Ages roads were no-man's-land, and travelers were exposed to robbers. Gurevich (1972, 165) writes that the most one could expect to cover on horseback in 24 hours was a few dozen kilometers, while pedestrians moved even more slowly on the wretched roads. For example, the journey from Bologna to Avignon took up to two weeks, from Nîmes to the Champagne trade-fairs took 22 days, and even to get from Florence to Naples took 11 or 12 days.

A letter from Pope Gregory VII, written in Rome on December 8, 1075, reached Goslar in the Harz on January 1, 1076. News of the death of Frederick Barbarossa in Asia Minor reached Germany four months later, and it took four weeks for the English to learn that King Richard the

Lionheart had been taken prisoner in Austria. The courier run from Rome to Canterbury normally took up to seven weeks, but especially urgent news could be delivered in four weeks (Gurevich 1972, 43–44). As a consequence, people went on living their lives without any knowledge of "notable events" that had happened much earlier.

Special couriers were used to carry tidings. Commercial correspondence developed between the major cities in the thirteenth century. There is evidence that from 1260 a regular and dependable courier service had come into existence between the commercial centers of Tuscany and the fairs of Champagne (Spufford 2002, 25). As Spufford writes, running a regular courier service was an expensive business:

> It involved not only the payment and maintenance of an adequately sized group of couriers for each route, but also access to an enormous number of horses, which had to be available for frequent changes of mount at suitable intervals all along the routes. (Spufford 2002, 25)

Holl writes that at the turn of the twelfth to thirteenth centuries "something began to stir in Europe. More than eight hundred years ago, people in some European cities began to feel a strange and previously unheard-of desire. They wanted to know the time" (Nowotny 1994, 16). God's time, as Le Goff put it, was giving way to the time of the traders and written news – in the form of newsletters – was beginning to manifest in Renaissance Europe as it had in Rome and in China (Stephens 1988, 73).

These newsletters also needed to be carried, though. By the early fifteenth century there were several important regular courier services. In the early 1420s the commercial couriers from Florence were expected to reach agents in Rome, nearly 300 km away, in five or six days; agents in Naples, nearly 500 km away, in 11 days; agents in Paris in 20 to 22 days; those in Bruges, nearly 1,400 km distant, in under 25 days, and those in Seville, nearly 2,000 km away, in under 32 days (Spufford 2002, 27).

Walking "newsmen" appeared in public places in big cities where people expected to hear news in exchange for a coin, similar to the *gazetta* on the Rialto Bridge. In Paris during the sixteenth century there existed about 15,000 *nouvellistes* or walking newsmen, some of them in the Tuileries; in other cities they worked near markets or in the harbour area (Stangerup 1973/1974, 25–26). Gathering points for newsmongers in London were behind St Paul's; during the first half of the seventeenth-century news writers used to meet near Westminster (Höyer 2003, 452).

Smith points out the improvement of the mail service in the seventeenth century. By the second half of the century, letters could be passed between Amsterdam and Paris in six days by the ordinary mail and in two days by a more expensive service. Most communication with London depended on twice-weekly packets but express communication was also available at a price (Smith 1984, 991). Postmasters were often correspondents in a network of news exchanges, comparable to more modern news bureaux. From about 1600, postmasters in European cities collected news from their own districts and mailed it to centers such as Hamburg, Paris, or London where it was edited and redistributed (Hart 1970, 13). Copenhagen was a news center for Scandinavia. Sensitive items which could not be published at home could sometimes be published abroad. Thus, demonstrations in Stockholm in January 1783 were reported in French, but not in Swedish newspapers, even though the reporter was Swedish (Höyer 2003, 452).

As Höyer writes, in telling stories about unknown or only partly known events, the newspaper was preceded by flysheets, pamphlets, printed ballads, and songs, and by political prints, handbills, and other printed ephemera. Overlap in content between newspapers, periodicals, and other forms of printed propaganda were quite common. When the first printed news-sheets appeared they were almost exact copies of the hand-written newsletters: the same short information, the notices and two-liners, and the same random distribution of content (Höyer 2003, 452).

Printed News

In the seventeenth century ballads were replaced by news books or pamphlets (Davis 1983, 71). Davis (1983, 50) notes that *facts* and *newes* could be mutually exclusive categories. The word *newes* was applied freely to writings which described either true or fictional events, quotidian or supernatural occurrences, and affairs that may have been recent or several decades old.

Davis (1980, 120) writes that the authors of English *novels* of the seventeenth and early eighteenth centuries always began their works with a preface asserting that they were presenting *not* a fiction but a *factual account of some real series of events* (my emphasis). Even in ballads, the words *novel*, *newes*, and *new* are used interchangeably. Ballads always claimed to be new and were sold for their newness (Davis 1983, 48–51). The word "newes" was also used to describe books written in prose which reported on foreign news and noteworthy occurrences. Titles like *A Sack Full of News* (1557), *News from Antwerp* (1580), and *News from Hell* (1606) reveal differing degrees of factuality, ranging from jest-book to news ballad to religious-satirical commentary (Davis 1980, 126). Davis concludes (1980, 127) that during the sixteenth and seventeenth centuries novels and news reports were not seen as clearly fictional or as clearly factual; narrative during this time seemed to be categorized in ways that were not dependent on the distinction between fact and fiction. In other words, news could be novels, and novels could be news.

Davis (1983, 58) also observes that, with the advent of journalism, the temporal distance between reader and event is bridged by the technology of instantaneous dispersal of news – which makes possible a relatively small temporal gap between reader and event. As Harris writes, "by the 1690s, the culture, at least in big cities, became so obsessed with the potential significance to human consciousness of any single moment that an imme-diate written record needed to be created, and the preoccupations with news and novelty in fact coalesced" (Harris 1990, 172). Distances started to collapse: between the 1760s and the end of the century the journey from London to Glasgow was shortened from between 10 and 12 days to 62 hours. The system of mail-coaches or diligences instituted in the second half of the eighteenth century was even faster – the postal service from Paris to Strasbourg took 36 hours in 1833 (Hobsbawm 1975, 9). The invention of the printing press made newspapers more regular, but their delivery was still often dependent on transportation by foot, ship, or horse. News was not new in the modern understanding of the word, but it became regular and anticipated. News was in fact still old: days, weeks, or even months old, especially if arriving from a distance. But it was new in the sense that it was not previously known, no matter how far back in the past it originated, and at the same time new because it was labeled as news and published in a special section for news.

A Swedish-language newspaper, *Tidningar utgifne af et sällskap I Åbo*, published in Åbo in Finland in March 1773 a letter that had been sent from London in February of that year. These travelers' letters were an early form of foreign news. Increasingly, newspapers also published foreign news "borrowed" from other newspapers. Swedish newspapers arrived in Finland when they were at least a day or two, if not a week or two, old. The average age of foreign news in *Tidningar utgifne af et sällskap i Åbo* varied from six days (from St Petersburg) to four months (from Cape Town) (Rantanen 1987, 58).

The situation was not much different elsewhere in Europe. News of the outcome of the battle of Trafalgar, where the British fleet beat the French and Spanish fleets and Admiral Nelson died on October 12, 1805 reached London only on November 6. News of the defeat of Napoleon at Austerlitz on December 2, 1805 reached newspaper readers 17 days later. News of the death of Napoleon on St Helena on May 5, 1821 was published in *The Times* only two months later, on July 4 (Höhne 1977, 21).

Sometimes transport by sea was not only faster, but easier and cheaper than by road. As Hobsbawm (1975, 9) observes, it took Goethe, during his Italian tour of 1786–1788, four days to sail from Naples to Sicily and three days to sail back. To be within reach of a port was to be within reach of the world: in a real sense London was closer to Plymouth than to villages in the Breckland of Norfolk (Hobsbawm 1975, 9). But transport by sea was not always smooth, and a place that was closer in distance was sometimes further in terms of time taken to receive news. This is evident from the first foreign news published in 1847 in *Suometar*, a Finnish-language newspaper in Helsinki, then in the Grand Duchy of Finland in Imperial Russia, but also a neighbor of Sweden separated from that country only by the Baltic Sea (Rantanen 1987, 51):

> In *Turkey* the Sultan, alias the Emperor, has been quite busy improving the government's faults and assisting enlightenment. – In *Persia* and further to the East the cholera has killed mercilessly. – On the northern side of *India* the English have been messing with the odd clans of Asia. – From *Sweden* there is no news because the sea is frozen and prevents the mail getting through.

Hobsbawm (1975, 10) writes that the chief drawback of water transport was its intermittent nature. Even in 1820, the London mail consignments for Hamburg and Holland were made up only twice a week, those for Sweden and Portugal once a week and those for North America once a month (Hobsbawm 1975, 10). Most information was hand-written and carried by mail.

There was also a mixture of many different kinds of communication. Oral communication was mixed with every new form of communication – script or printed. Darnton points out the mixture of different kinds of communication in pre-revolutionary Paris.

Darnton's model (Figure 1.1) shows how different forms of communications existed simultaneously and complemented each other. There were

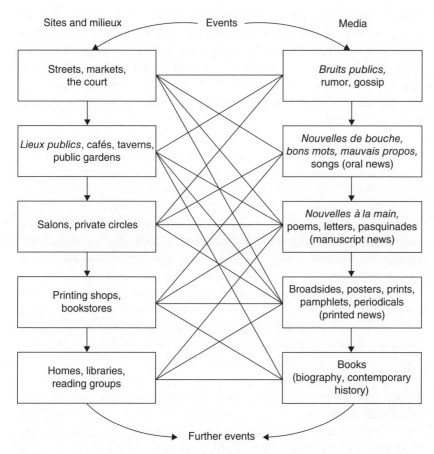

Figure 1.1 A schematic model of a communication circuit (Darnton 1995, 189).

several circuits that partly overlapped but partly lived their separate lives. In their separateness they also started to form new and distinctive categories of stories.

Electronic News

Time-place compression began radically to change with the introduction from the mid-nineteenth century of the telegraph and of submarine cables. Electronic news began to travel by itself and at the speed of electricity – no longer with a messenger along winding roads or across stormy seas, but along direct lines and almost instantaneously. Of course, telegraph lines and submarine cables could be cut, preventing the *transmission* of messages, and these messages did not reach every corner of the globe, but the change was by any standards drastic. As Smith observes, the telegraph made possible the idea that a newspaper's coverage should encompass the events of a *day*. He writes

> Such boundaries hardly correspond with the conceptual and cognitive categories accepted elsewhere, but henceforth daily journalism operated in a new tense, as it were, of the *instantaneous* present. (Smith 1978, 167, my emphasis)

The telegraph also made it possible to send the same message to several locations simultaneously and thus to multiply it endlessly. The global mass-production of news began with the telegraph and the foundation of the first news (telegraph) agencies. Paradoxically, this made the delivery of electronic news more complicated, because a more distinct separation now emerged between the gatherers, producers, and users of news. A news-gatherer was like a coalminer, gathering the raw material (information) from which news was manufactured and then sold to clients. In fact, this was the beginning of the industrialization of news.

In most countries, the telegraph lines were built along railway lines. Hence, speedier transportation was closely combined with speedier transmission, although these were now separate. The introduction of railways, and thus of the telegraph, resulted in the increasing standardization of time, thus adding to the value of news, whose newness could now be measured not only in days, as in the pre-telegraph era, but in hours and minutes.

Before the railways were introduced each location or region operated on its own time, taken from solar readings. The promotion of uniform time made possible the introduction of railway timetables. Before this there were about 60 different railway times in the United States alone (Kern 1983, 12). Greenwich time was universally adopted in 1887. Universal time contributed mainly in two ways to perceived value of time in news: (1) by giving a timetable of news and (2) by creating additional value for news in different time zones.

Every single news story could now be datelined not only with the day but also with the hour. By 1860 the telegraph could handle 10 words per minute, by 1900 about 150 words per minute and by 1920 about 400. By 1900, orders from London to buy or sell could reach the New York Stock

Exchange in three minutes (McNeill and McNeill 2003, 218). Competition for the latest news became more intensive, as who received it first and was able to deliver it faster to the customer became a question only of hours, then of minutes and seconds. The news agencies were compared to each other in terms of their capacity to transmit the latest news and to provide a constant flow of news almost without interruption. Day or night, working day or holiday, news had to flow constantly and steadily. "Today we have no news" became unthinkable.

The adoption of time zones meant that the same news could be re-labeled as the latest news in different time zones. When electronic news overcame distance and was able to be transmitted instantaneously around the world, it gained an additional value, since news could be sold several times over in different time zones, with what was already old news in London, for example, being still new in New York. This was also true, of curse, with any new stories, but the introduction of time zones could be further used to make news new by creating the sense of universally measured time that connected people together in different locations around the world.

In the early days of the telegraph, transportation by sea and transmission by telegraph were combined. President Lincoln was assassinated on April 14, 1865 in New York. It took 12 days to transport the news by the steamship *Nova Scotia* to the telegraph station at Greencastle, near Londonderry, in the north of Ireland. By 11.30 a.m. on April 26 a message from Reuters – datelined New York, April 15, 9 a.m. – reached the offices of the London newspapers which published it on April 27: "President Lincoln was shot by an assassin last night, and died this morning. An attempt was likewise made to assassinate Mr Seward, and he is not expected to live" (Read 1999, 43). The sense of newness was skilfully constructed in this datelined story. The fact that President Lincoln had died 13 days earlier did not matter, since the news item spoke of "last night" and "this morning." It was still news in London, although the actual event had taken place much earlier, but by giving its readers the datelines the new story was made the latest news.

The increasingly widespread transmission of news by cable, replacing transportation by steamship, resulted in an immediate change in the speed of its delivery. On August 1, 1866 the first hard same-day news was telegraphed to London – the resignation of the US Secretary of the Interior. The 12 days taken in 1865 for news of Lincoln's assassination to reach London became unacceptable, and the first news in 1881 of the shooting of President Garfield appeared in the London papers within 24 hours of the event. In consequence much more extensive mourning was observed in Britain for Garfield than had been the case for Lincoln (Read 1999, 96–97).

However, distance and the overcoming of distance by time affect news in several ways. First, the event which the news is about is new because it took place recently and was reported soon after. Second, the news itself may be new even if the event is old, because the audience did not previously know about it. It follows that a new event may become old news if it has already been reported, and old news may become new if it has not yet reached an audience. The third aspect of temporality in news lies in the impossibility of *no news*, of "no novelty, nothing new",[2] which implies the wider influence of news in society, emphasizing the importance of news in establishing social time.

The new form of industrially produced timely news was not universally accepted. Nerone and Barnhurst (2001, 435) write that it was Horace Greeley, editor of a leading newspaper, the *New York Tribune*, who, in 1845, predicted that the telegraph would take over newsgathering, outsourcing it from the newspaper and allowing the newspaper to devote its energies instead to the philosophical work of making sense of the news. Within a short time, however, according to Greeley, the consensus became the opposite. The telegraph, and allied developments in local reporting, had turned the newspaper into an ever more ephemeral miscellany of bizarre events. Another contemporary of Greeley, Charles Dudley Warner, argued in 1881 that both telegraph operators and reporters had a bias toward volume – being paid by the piece, they wanted to produce as much as possible – and toward the sensational. "Our newspapers every day are loaded with accidents, casualties, and crime concerning people of whom we never heard before and never shall hear again, the reading of which is of no earthly use to any human being." Nerone and Barnhurst conclude that the *industrial* newspaper, focused as it was on the ever more routinized production of news, did not take on the task of interpreting it, and the editors who managed reporters discouraged them from doing so (Nerone and Barnhurst 2001, 435).

When News Became New

The elements of which news is made up are events, sources, and information. When news is manufactured as a good it is temporalized and localized in the narrative form of a story that is socially recognizable as news. The narrative form of news at a given time varies considerably both historically and geographically.

Information becomes a news story only when it is narrativized and exchanged. Information can be stored and kept for further purposes, but is not news unless its novelty is recognized. In oral communication, information is stored inside one's head and memorized. Until it is shared with somebody, it remains just information. When it is exchanged with somebody who did not know about it and who acknowledges its novelty, it becomes a new story. Anybody might store information about a range of things, from concrete to abstract, but an organized exchange of new stories as an everyday experience changed information into new stories. Anybody might also be a source, because, in oral communication, people simply talk to each other and mostly exchange new stories freely. The exchange of new stories often concentrates on an event, but also on a comment or a re-comment about an event.

When new stories were "old," as they were in ballads or songs, they were still "new" because they consisted of new information, of something that was not previously known. The source had to know how to deliver new stories in such a way that they were recognizable as new. With the advent of the printing press, there was at first no differentiation between what was a news story and what was a "novel," but this distinction gradually began to appear when books and papers became separate. Simultaneously, news became more "factual," while the novel became more "fictional." When newspapers published news, it was not necessarily "new," but the timing, regularity, and increasing frequency of their appearance made news "newer." Still, the event could sometimes be "old"; there could be a spatial and temporal distance between the event and the information, but the publication and the narrative made it "new," i.e., news.

The telegraph profoundly changed the concept of time, not only nationally but also globally. Most scholars acknowledge the role of *communications* technology, such as the telegraph, but pay less attention to the role of *media*. Simultaneously, news became ephemeral, a perishable commodity that was no longer memorized, as new stories had been, but easily forgotten. News has to be repeated more frequently, because it loses its value with time. When the number of news increased, they had to be printed and stored because it became impossible to memorize news. Newspapers turned new stories into news by developing a new genre of writing that was labeled as news because of its temporality.

The new product, electronic news, the combination of the "lightness" of the telegraph and the "heaviness" of the information content, resulted in new features of immediacy and temporality. Because news had to be new and thus immediate, it gained a value of temporality which was something of a two-edged sword, becoming eminently saleable but also easily perishable. Electronic news had a very short life: it was like a mayfly, living for several months underwater as a larva before emerging for a brief life as a winged adult.[5] The mass-production of news meant that the production process became longer than it had been, although transmission became shorter, and that the finished product had a very short life.

Source, place, and time became important identifications of what makes news new. Together they framed the event the news was about. Equally, news started to mark time: there were certain times when the audience expected to receive news, whether by reading a newspaper in the morning or later listening to radio news or watching television. An individual had to wait for news that was chosen for him/her by a medium. News reminded its audience that it was time for news.

The temporal aspects in news have changed drastically since news was "invented." We see a gradual change, an evolution from oral news into electronic news. Every form of new technology has changed the form of news but at the same time used some aspects if its earlier forms. The change has never been a complete departure from the old: the old forms have existed with the latest ones. Together they have contributed to the increasing temporalization of news that exceeds its influence over news to contemporary societies. However, as will be further discussed in Chapter Seven, our understanding of news is primarily based on the nineteenth-century concept of electronic news.

Notes

1   http://dictionary.oed.com/, last visited October 27, 2008.
2   http://dictionary.oed.com/, last visited October 27, 2008.

2

Cosmopolitanization

An Older Phenomenon Than We Think

Hence the representative of the modern world in the list of examples of metageographies [. . .] – the map of nation-states – is not the metageography of the whole of the history of the modern-world system. In the modern world there has been more than one metageography. (Taylor 2004, 191)

Although many academics have acknowledged that there is a strong connection between cities and the media (for example Park 1922; Park et al. 1967), media and communications studies often take the nation-state as *the* natural starting point for any analysis. Partly this has to do with the periodization they adopt. Many authors (for example Chalaby 1998; Schudson 1978) argue that modern journalism was invented in the latter half of the nineteenth century in the United States. Coincidentally, this was also the period of high nationalism and it is not surprising that both news and its study are easily nationalized. As a result, we now take for granted that news and the news organizations that produce it (for example, news agencies) have a nationality (for example Sreberny-Mohammadi et al. 1985).

For decades, most research on news has been carried out within the categories of either the "international" or the "national," and both categories have been left unproblematized. This is, as Beck says, an "either or" rather than a "both and" approach (Rantanen 2005, 257) which ignores other spatial levels and simplifies their mutual interdependences and complexities. In this chapter I argue that the division into the international and the national has prevented us from seeing how early news was a product of *cosmopolitan* cities rather than of nation-states.

In many academic fields, such as geography and sociology, researchers have already focused on the role of cities in global networks (for example Braudel 1979/1984; Castells 1989; Sassen 1991/2001; Taylor 2004). This has not been the case in media studies, although cities are particularly interesting as an object of study for media and communications scholars. Research on media and communications not only reveals their importance in the formation and maintenance of cities, but also underlines their crucial role in the networks between the cities. These networks contribute to globalization, which is often defined by increasing interconnectivity.

Theories of globalization challenge established methodological practices and paradigms, notably that of the nation-state as the starting point for research (Giddens 1990; Robertson 1992; Appadurai 1990). Castells's (1996) network theory offers a different account of salient contemporary social relationships (but one compatible with globalization): he proposes that established hierarchical social and political structures have given way to networks. These networks (and here is the major intersection with globalization theories) are non-isomorphic with nation-states. Together, these new concepts signify a change in social scientific heuristic paradigms, but this shift has not yet been echoed in the study of global news flows.

Furthermore, media and communications scholars are interested not only in transmission technology, but also in content. News is of particular importance because it is an early information product. However, media and communications studies have almost entirely "nationalized" news by studying it nearly exclusively within a national framework, and have ignored cities as starting points. As Stephens (1988, 151) writes, cities that were centers of power and trade were also centers of news. As a result, early news was cosmopolitan rather than national.

Sassen reminds us that it took centuries of struggle, wars, treaties made, and treaties broken to *nationalize* territories along mutually exclusive lines and secure the distinctive concentration of power and system of rule that is now the sovereign state. She writes

> Multiple systems of rules coexisted during the transition from the medieval system of rule to the modern state: there were centralizing monarchies in Western Europe, city-states in Italy, and city-leagues in Germany. Even when nation-states with exclusive territoriality and sovereignty were beginning to emerge, other forms might have become effective alternatives – for example, the Italian city-states and the Hanseatic League in northern Europe – and the formation of and claims by central states were widely contested. (Sassen 1996, 3)

Fields (2004, 11) notes that the communication revolution is connected to territorial transformation. His idea is not new, since it has been argued that communication revolutions have resulted in territorial and spatial transformations in the context of empires (Innis 1950/1972) or nations (Eisenstein 1979/2005), but not of cities. Innis and Eisenstein emphasize that the introduction and use of communication technology – the transformation from oral to script, from script to printing, from printing to electronic communication – have changed the ways in which we exert control over time and space.

Innis famously divided the media into time- and space-biased. Time-biased media include hand-written and oral sources that are long-lasting, but whose spatial extension is limited. Space-biased media include most of the modern media, such as radio and television, as well as newspapers. As Innis observes, the advent of printing on paper facilitated an effective development of the vernaculars and gave expression to their vitality in the growth of nationalism (Innis 1950/1972, 170, 176). While time-biased media favoured communities, space-biased media favoured imperialism. Carey (1998, 31) writes that "this imperialism of images spread the representation of the national into all geographic times and spaces and into all cultural times and spaces as well." According to Gillespie and Robins, Innis recognized that space-biased media and communications encouraged the centralization of power and control over space. This realization was at the heart of Innis's concern for the "problem of empire" (Gillespie and Robins 1989, 9).

It is now time to formulate a new argument about the role of new media and communications in territorial transformations, by introducing cities as a new level of analysis and news as not only technology but information goods. This requires the introduction of a new concept that connects news, cities, and globalization: cosmopolitanization.

Terminology

Braudel, in his seminal book *Perspective of the World* (1979/1984), uses the term *world city* to underline the role of European cities in a world-economy. For him, a world-economy has "always an urban centre of gravity, a city, as the logistics of its activity." He also focuses on news, pointing out that "news, merchandise, capital, credit, people, instructions, correspondence all flow into and out of the city" (1979/1984, 27). In 1500 there were only four cities in Europe with populations of more than 100,000, but by 1800 there were 23. One of these, London had more than a million inhabitants (Burke 1994, 244).

Table 2.1   The population of London and of England compared

Year	Population of London	Population of England	% in London
1600	200,000	4,100,000	4.9
1630	400,000	4,900,000	8.2
1700	575,000	5,000,000	11.5
1750	675,000	5,800,000	11.6
1801	900,000	8,300,000	10.8

Source: Hunter 1990, 112.

Braudel's approach is accordingly *longue durée*. He defines as historical world cities Venice, Antwerp, Amsterdam, London, and New York, which over time dominated and then replaced one other. He writes (1979/1984, 32)

> Venice was replaced by Antwerp that was replaced by Amsterdam that was replaced by London that was replaced by New York [...] When Amsterdam replaced Antwerp, when London took over from Amsterdam or when, in about 1929, New York overtook London, it always meant a massive historical shift of forces, revealing the precariousness of the previous equilibrium and the strengths of the one which was replacing it.

Unlike Braudel, Castells explores the role of contemporary cities. He (Castells 1989, 343) sees the dependence upon telecommunications networks that requires the concentration of command and control centers in spaces that are provided with the most advanced systems, as being key elements in a contemporary *informational city*. Sassen (1994, 19) defines contemporary *global* cities as key sites for the advanced services and telecommunications facilities necessary for the implementation and management of global economic operations. Both refer to these new types of city as recent phenomena that appeared in the latter part of the twentieth century with the *new informational economy*. These cities emblemize the new information-based mode of production, in contrast to the earlier *industrial mode of production* (Castells 1989, 12). I recognize the value of Sassen's and Castells's concept, but in this chapter use the concept of a cosmopolitan city to pinpoint the role of cities in the early phase of the globalization of the media.

Chalaby (2005, 28–32) has distinguished three phases in global media transition. The first is the *internationalization* of the media that started in the nineteenth century when the first international markets emerged with the coming of the telegraph and submarine cables. The second, the *globalization* of the media, took place from the 1960s with innovations in telecommunications and computing and the emergence of a few global companies with a global reach. The third is the *transnationalization* of the media, when market and audiences have become de-nationalized with the emergence and use of new media. Chalaby sees *cosmopolitanization* as a distinctive feature of the third period.

In this chapter I argue, that the cosmopolitanization of news preceded its internationalization (see also Rantanen 2006b) which has now been challenged by globalization. I also argue, in contrast to earlier research on the relationship between "national" and international' news, that the first European electronic news agencies were *not* originally "national" or "international," but rather cosmopolitan, exchanging news between cities – a tradition already established in Europe centuries before.

Cosmopolitan Cities

Rather than the concept of a world-global, or informational city, I use that of a *cosmopolitan* city to pinpoint the role of cities in the *early* phase of the cosmopolitanization of the media (Rantanen 2006b) that took place before the internationalization and globalization of the media. Numerous authors have referred to the cosmopolitan character of many of the leading cities of the past. Braudel (1979/1984, 30) writes that "Under the pillars of the Amsterdam Bourse – which was a microcosm of the world of trade – one would hear every dialect in the world. In Venice, if you are curious to see men from every part of the earth, each dressed in his own different way, go to St Mark's Square or the Rialto and you will find all manner of persons" (Braudel 1979/1984, 30). He also refers to the tolerant atmosphere, and especially the religious tolerance, in these cities. In London, for example, every religion under the sun was practiced (Braudel 1979/1984, 31). According to Nicholas (2003, 186–187), the size and diversity of the population of Antwerp, including religious dissidents in exile – many English religious works of the 1520s and 1530s were printed in Antwerp and smuggled into England – was a major contributing factor in the success of printing in that city. Eisenstein (1979/2005, 336–337) writes that

More histories of printing follow the convention of organizing developments around the rise of the major nation-states. The procedure works well enough for nineteenth-century developments, but it is likely to skew patterns when applied to the earlier, more cosmopolitan age of the handpress. The major centers of book production down through the eighteenth century were *not* congruent with the major political capitals such as Paris, Berlin, Vienna, Rome, Madrid and London. They were, rather, great commercial centers such as Venice, Antwerp and Amsterdam. [. . .] The central city for the French language press of the eighteenth century was not Paris; it was Amsterdam.

The inhabitants of the cosmopolitan city tend to be cosmopolitans (for example Hannerz 1996; Beck 2002) with a knowledge of several languages, access to and familiarity with the latest communications technology, a sense of freedom from restriction to one place and of belonging to several places. These characteristics have been understood as primarily related to socio-economic status, which they often are. But, as this chapter will show, the same characteristics can be found in individuals who resist the existing world order and are critical of it. They are not necessarily members of the dominant elite, indeed are often excluded from that elite by their ethnicity, ideology, or religion. By establishing links with other places, cosmopolitans cosmopolitanize those places also. They bring the world into cities.

Many researchers have recently raised the issue of cosmopolitanism in their analysis of contemporary societies. However, the concept is also useful in historical analysis. Hannerz (1996, 129–131) writes of contemporary cities, distinguishing the presence of four categories as necessary to the formation of a cosmopolitan city: (1) transnational business; (2) third world populations; (3) artists and artisans; and (4) tourists.

If New York, London, or Paris are not merely localized manifestations of American, British, or French culture, or even peculiarly urban versions of them, but something qualitatively different, it is in very large part due to the presence of these four categories. What they have in common is the fact that they are in one way or another transnational; the people involved are physically present in the world cities for some larger or smaller part of their lives, but they have also strong ties to some other place in the world.

All four of Hannerz's categories, I would argue, could equally be found in cities in earlier centuries. For the purpose of analyzing the formation of cosmopolitan cities, I would add migrants and political refugees, although these can be present within other categories. However, what was further required in earlier times was a certain degree of unruliness, i.e., what Eisenstein (1979/2005, 337) calls "the absence of any powerful central authority," such as a nation-state.

Written News

The exchange of news was always and is still vital for cities. According to Smith (1979, 18–19), since the Middle Ages a formal network of correspondents and intelligence agents had come into being in European cities, sending news of military, diplomatic, and ecclesiastical affairs along a series of prescribed routes. The first *gazettes*, hand-written newsletters distributed every week, were produced in Venice in 1550 (Stephens 1988, 152). Politicians, courtiers, and merchants who were particularly anxious to know what was going on abroad established a regular correspondence with their friends and agents in important cities and were thus kept *au courant* with the kind of events they needed information about (Shaaber 1929, 2). As Eisenstein (1979/2005, 338) observes, the far-flung networks and sophisticated systems of financing developed by the late medieval merchants were already available for the spread of printed products. News, whether oral or hand-written, traveled with messengers along these routes.

The wealthy merchant House of Fugger invested in its own system for the collection of *hand-written* news (1568–1605) primarily for its own family and business associates. The majority of reports, according to Stephens (1988, 76), concerned the procession of battles, disasters, plots, miracles, royal births, deaths, marriages, and financial news, including insolvencies at the Antwerp Exchange. Braudel (1979/1984, 143–145) points out that the age of Fugger was actually the age of Antwerp as the center of the entire international economy. Antwerp was cosmopolitan, since it did not have its own native merchants of international standing. As a result, foreigners dominated the scene – Hanseatic traders, English, French, and above all southern merchants: Portuguese, Spanish, and Italian. Antwerp had a large printing establishment even before the advent of the printing house of Christopher Plantin (1514–1589), a migrant from France (Nicholas 2003, 186).

However, the flow of news in Renaissance Europe was still intimately connected to transportation, with the mail service developing from the late fifteenth century. A distinction was commonly made between ordinary newsletters – which had been sent by the *regular*, usually *weekly*, mail – and *extraordinary* newsletters – something akin to newspaper supplements, sent by special messenger (Stephens 1988, 76–77). According to Sardella their arrival created a new global sensibility. Sardella writes:

> Through the news they shared, the wheat traders of Venice, the silver traders of Antwerp, the merchants of Nuremberg, the financiers of Augsburg, and their trading partners around the world, were being drawn together into a society based on this new sensibility; on common interests – the fate of some ships sailing from India to Lisbon; on common values – a belief in the rights of capital. (Stephens 1988, 77)

The Printing Press and the Early Printed News

By 1600 the demand for more information had reached the level at which it had become economic to find the printed means for distributing it. The technology needed to industrialize news transmission was the printing press. It was one of the earliest industrial technologies: apart from printing and metalworking, there were few fundamental changes in industrial technology before the Industrial Revolution. Except for printing, little urban industry developed before about 1500 (Nicholas 2003, 22, 51).

The invention of the Gutenbergian press around 1450 made possible the mechanical printing of the first books and then of newspapers. By 1500, 236 towns in Europe had Gutenberg-style presses (McNeill and McNeill 2003, 180). These towns, were also connected to each other. Franz von Taxis (1459–1517) was the first to establish a well-organized postal network in Italy and laid the foundation-stone for the development of an international postal system. The Thurn und Thaxis mail system covered most of Western Europe and was thus in contact with the mailmen of every European town. For example, correspondence between Innsbruck and Brussels could be accomplished within five days.[1] The Fugger merchant house continued to maintain correspondents throughout Europe and the mail seems to have got through in almost all circumstances. For example, at the end of a dispatch from Antwerp dated May 31, 1586, Fugger's Antwerp agent describes events at a turbulent time, but ends: "Letters from London arrive daily by post notwithstanding, and letters are being sent there from here without any hindrance" (Beale 2005, 240).

The new printing presses had a distinctive cosmopolitan character. The printers themselves moved across Europe in search of new towns in which concessions could be obtained for periodicals (Smith 1979, 25). For example, the first printers in Paris were Germans; although they did not print for the university, they published classical texts and grammars that had a market among the students and masters (Nicholas 2003, 186). Eisenstein (1997, 23) writes:

> Their shops were different from those run by other contemporary manufacturers because they served as gathering places for scholars, artists and literati; as sanctuaries for foreign translators, émigrés and refugees; as institutions of advanced learning, and as focal points for every kind of cultural and intellectual interchange.

New weekly newspapers spread fastest in German cities and in Amsterdam and other cities in the Low Countries that had well-worked links across Europe and the known world (Smith 1979, 17). By 1610 there appears to have been a printed weekly in Basel, by 1615 in Frankfurt and Vienna, by 1616 in Hamburg, by 1617 in Berlin, by 1618 in Amsterdam, and by 1620 in Antwerp (Stephens 1988, 150). There were 57 newspapers published in German in 1701 (Black 2001, 21). Before 1626 there are known to have been 140 separate news publications in Dutch, many of these also appearing in various other languages, including English and French, and intended for sale throughout Europe. The first *corantos* (newsbooks or newspapers) in English were shipped across the North Sea from Amsterdam to London in 1620 (Smith 1979, 17). In 1644 Londoners could choose from a dozen weekly newsbooks composed of eight or more pages, and during the early 1650s eight long-running weeklies were on sale in London (Harris 1978, 83). The early newspapers were bearers of general information: a compilation of political and economic news (Smith 1984, 999), and almost exclusively foreign news (Stephens 1988, 165).

Smith (1984, 987) argues that it was precisely the nature of information as a commodity and as a by-product of the operations of the trade networks that led in the seventeenth century to the evolution in Amsterdam of a central information exchange for the whole of Europe. He shows six different channels through which *business* data flowed: (1) private merchant correspondence; (2) institutional correspondence; (3) movement of businessmen to and from Amsterdam; (4) consular reports; (5) diplomatic reports; and (6) special channels (Smith 1984, 990).

The first printing press arrived in England in 1476 (Stephens 1988, 67). By 1663, London could boast of 11 mail deliveries per day (Rifkin 1987, 145). The oldest surviving *coranto* ("current," "running") printed in London is from 1621: *Corante, or weekly newes from Italy, Germany, Hungary, Poland, Bohemia, France and the Low Countreys* (Stephens 1988, 161). The first regular newspaper was founded in 1702 in London, and in 1760 London had four dailies and five or six tri-weeklies, in 1770 at least five dailies, eight tri-weeklies and ten bi- or three-weeklies. Their respective volumes were: in 1764, 1,090,289, in 1782, 3,070,000 and in 1790, 4,650,000 copies. By 1780, there were 13 morning, one evening and seven tri-weekly and two bi-weekly papers. In 1811, the total number of papers in all categories published in London was 52 (Smith 1979, 52, 56–57; Black 2001, 74). There was also collective access: in London there were 559 coffee houses in business, and most found it necessary to offer a selection of newspapers to their customers (Harris 1978, 90–91). As early as 1667, a London broadside, *News from the Coffe-House*, satirized the phenomenon (Harris 1990, 174):

> You that delight in Wit and Mirth
> And long to hear such News
> As comes from all Parts of the Earth . . .
> Go hear it at the Coffe House
> It cannot be true.

As Barker (2000, 57) writes, for the price of a drink, coffee houses and public houses provided easy access to newspapers for those who could not afford to buy their own. Literacy was at that time seen as both an individual and a collective skill, and those who could read were expected to serve as readers for those who could not (Vincent 1989, 23). It was estimated that every newspaper copy was "read" by at least 20 people (Barker 2000, 46).

Telegraph News

In Central and Western Europe, some cities, such as London, Berlin, Paris, and Vienna, gained a further important function from the late 1830s onwards, becoming the focal point of a rapidly expanding railway network

Table 2.2 Some early commercial and public telegraph lines and submarine cables in Europe, 1839–1853.

1839 Paddington (London)–West Drayton (commercial line, 13 miles)
1841 London–Slough
1845 London–Gosport (public line)
1845 Paris–Rouen
1846 Berlin–Potsdam
1847 Berlin–Breslau–Vienna
1848 Berlin–Frankfurt-am-Main–Cologne
1849 Aix-la-Chapelle (Aachen)–Berlin
1850 Paris–Brussels–Berlin

(Hachtmann 2001, 345). Since telegraph lines were built along railway lines, it was no coincidence that the countries that had the most developed telegraph network were exactly these same countries (Heimbürger 1938, 12; Briggs and Burke 2005, 112–113). For example, by 1850 there were 2,215 miles of telegraph wire in Britain. By 1852, there was a network of 1,493 miles of wire in Prussia, radiating out of Berlin (Standage 1998, 61–62). The early telegraphs, connecting point-to-point, enabled railways to run to planned schedules; they also connected stock exchanges: the London and Paris exchanges were connected in 1851 (Cherry 1977, 115). The completion of the first telegraph lines across borders further underlined the importance of Paris, Berlin, and London as communication hubs in Europe.

The first users of the telegraph were often the stock exchanges located in major cities. However, the second group of users were newspapers. Never before had there been as many newspapers in Europe as there were in the years before the European revolutions of 1848. It was precisely in cities, in the centers of political and economic power, that the press exploded. In 1846, Paris (with over a million residents) had 26 dailies, with a total circulation of 180,000, that could be subscribed to, bought in the streets, or enjoyed in one of the countless reading circles, reading clubs, and cafés (Koch 2001, 600).

In Vienna, there were 181 periodicals, of all political currents, including 86 dailies. In Berlin, 135 different newspapers and journals arose between March 1848 and November 1849, including *National-Zeitung* (1848–1938) founded by Bernhard Wolff (Koch 2001, 586–601). The number of daily morning papers published in London was eight in 1856 and 21 in 1900. The equivalent numbers of evening papers were seven and 11 (Black 2001, 177). In 1854, the average circulation of a London daily was between 2,000 and 8,000, but *The Times* alone sold almost 60,000 copies (*Encyclopaedia Britannica* 1911a, 557). As Haupt and Langewiesche write, the political press permeated public life and helped to organize it. The formation of an inter-regional organization was dependent on a newspaper as a means of communication. The varied press landscape and the dense network of associations were closely woven together (Haupt and Langewiesche 2001, 6, 19).

The Founders of the First Telegraph Agencies

The founders of the early telegraph agencies in Europe, Messrs Havas, Reuter, and Wolff, were cosmopolitans of their time. As Slezkine (2004, 1) argues, the Jewish minorities, of all the many diasporic groups in the nineteenth century, were characterized by key qualities, such as being urban, mobile, literate, and articulate, which contributed to their success. Havas, Reuter, and Wolff were all Jewish, knew several languages, and tried several professions before becoming involved in the transmission of electronic news. Above all, they were not attached to only one country, but moved effortlessly across borders. They had some understanding of the latest technology, the telegraph, which they combined in the early days with carrier pigeons. They were located in the key European cities of that time: Berlin, London, and Paris. They knew something about publishing, journalism, and business: in short they were the dot.com businessmen of their age.

The oldest, Charles-Louis Havas (1783–1858), had lived in Portugal before settling in Paris. He was a bankrupted banker, who knew some Greek and Latin and spoke English and German fluently. Havas first bought a correspondence company, Correpondence Garnier. Founded in 1811, this had become in 1831 Bureau Börnstein, owned by a German political refugee who later left for the United States (Frédérix 1959, 13–19, Fuchs 1919, 11), and was delivering messages between Europe's major cities to diplomats, business people, and bankers. In 1832 Havas opened Bureau Havas (later Agence Havas) in the immediate neighborhood of the Post Office and

Exchange in Paris and started also to translate British, German, Spanish, Italian, and Russian newspapers and deliver these to other European cities. Before the telegraph lines were established, Havas started a pigeon service between London, Brussels, and Paris. The pigeons flew from London to Paris in six hours, and from Brussels to Paris in four hours. They left London at 8.00 a.m., bringing news from the morning papers that reached Paris at 2.00 in the afternoon (Fuchs 1919, 21–22).

Bernard Wolff (1811–1879) was a banker's son who became a medical doctor. Because of his father's bankruptcy, he never practiced his profession, but became a book publisher who translated medical books from English and French into German. Wolff started to work, with Paul Julius Reuter as his colleague, on publishing political pamphlets for Vossichen Buchhandlung in Berlin.

Reuter (1816–1899) was born Israel Beer Josaphat in Cassel, the son of a rabbi who changed his name and religion and worked as a bank clerk and book merchant in several cities, including Gotha and Berlin where he met Wolff. Together they left in 1848 for Paris (Basse 1991, 15).

Havas is said to have been the most conservative of the founders of the three first telegraph agencies in Europe (Hohenberg 1973, 8). He was a money lender to Napoleon who lost his money after Waterloo. It was no coincidence that the three met in Paris, the "capital of Europe" or "meeting place of Europe" and the starting point and center of a European revolution (Hachtmann 2001, 345). Since the revolution of 1848, "all eyes in Europe were watching that city where the revolution took place and the monarchy was abolished. Everybody wanted to experience the new, the latest and the most recent as soon as possible" (Fuchs 1919, 19). In contrast to Havas, Reuter and Wolff were involved in revolutionary activities in Berlin and had to flee in 1848 from there to Paris, where they started work in the Havas agency, located in the rooms of the Hotel de Bullion (Frédérix 1959, 21). Reuter worked as translator, but seems to have lacked any previous journalistic experience. Read writes that it may have been simply his command of German, French, and English (Read 1999, 9), but it was probably also his revolutionary contacts, that helped him, together with Wolff, to secure a job.

In Paris in 1848, while working in the Havas agency, Reuter also met Sigismund Engländer (1823–1902), a revolutionary journalist who had fled from Vienna to Paris under the threat of arrest and was working for Havas. Engländer was to become the chief architect of Reuters foreign correspondence network, a man whom Karl Marx described to Friedrich Engels as the heart and soul of the Reuter bureau, and who used his own revolutionary contacts to create a network of correspondents for Reuter (Read 1999, 30; Frédérix 1959, 77; Fuchs 1919, 11; Storey 1951, 3–17). Similarly, another revolutionary, Sigismund Kolisch, publisher of *Der Radikale*, escaped from Vienna to Paris and started working for Havas (Dörfler and Pensold 2001, 81).

After returning from Paris, Wolff became a newspaper publisher and his liberal paper *National-Zeitung* published its first telegram, on the subject of stock exchange prices from Frankfurt and Amsterdam, on November 27/28, 1849, with the following announcement (Fuchs 1919, 74; Höhne 1977, 44):

> To serve the interests of our readers we have decided not to ignore the latest communication technology, the telegraph. We have set up arrangements that allow us to transmit daily telegrams from Paris, London, Amsterdam and Frankfurt.

This service was then extended to other Berlin newspapers and private clients and became Telegraphisches Korrespondenz Bureau (B. Wolff), which started to transmit stock exchange information from London and Paris, and price information from Stettin, Frankfurt-am-Main, and Hamburg (Fuchs, 1919, 74).

Reuter stayed with Havas only until he had learned enough about telegraph agencies, and left in the spring of 1849 to open his own lithographic correspondence agency in a shabby room in the rue Jean-Jacques Rousseau, close to the main Paris Post Office and to Havas. He offered his services to newspapers all over Germany at very cheap rates, but there were not enough subscribers to make this viable. In the late summer of 1849, creditors seized Reuter's property and he moved to Aachen, where the telegraph line from Berlin had just been extended and opened to the public. Reuter's new firm became known as the Institut zur Beförderung Telegraphischer Depeschen (Institute for the Transmission of Telegraph Messages) and used pigeons to carry messages from Brussels to Aix-la-Chapelle/Aachen. After the telegraph line between Aachen and Brussels was completed Reuter had to move again, this time to London, where he opened an office in two rooms at 1 Royal Exchange Building, as near as possible to the Stock Exchange. Originally S. Josaphat and Co.'s Continental Telegraph, this became, in 1865, Reuters Telegram Company (Read 1999, 7–12).

The telegraph agencies were founded in Europe's key cities, where European capital, politics, and culture met. These cities were key places for networking – the places to be if one wanted to be connected to a wider world. The connections between these cities were not well developed in terms of speed, compared to contemporary global cities, since most messages had to be physically carried. It was the telegraph that started to connect them to one another. It is no coincidence that Havas, Reuter, and Wolff chose Paris, Berlin, and London as the locations of their agencies. Even Reuter, who started in Aix-la-Chapelle (later Aachen), soon realized that he had to move to a major capital. Because Wolff was already established in Berlin, he chose London.

The first telegraph agencies all contributed to the interconnectivity between Berlin, London, and Paris, establishing constant and immediate flows of political and financial news between these cities. By so doing, they also strengthened the position of these cities as key nodes in a new electronic global network. As their interconnections became faster and more regular, the positions of Paris, London, and Berlin became even stronger than before. The era of global electronic network society thus began with the establishment of the first telegraph agencies, exchanging messages between major cities.

Submarine Cables and News Agencies

Havas, Reuter, and Wolff made the first mutual agreement on the exchange of financial news in 1856, and this was then extended to political news (Rantanen 1990, 38). The first agreements concerned mainly cities in different countries, but were then extended to cover regions that crossed the boundaries of nation-states. The telegraph and submarine cables made possible the expansion of the telegraph network around the world. By 1876, over 200 submarine cables had been laid and succeeded in making virtually every corner of the earth a link in a worldwide chain of communications. Direct service could be conducted by telegraph between points several thousand miles apart. But the telegraph and submarine cables were like roads or railways: they had fixed nodes and routes. Even if lines and cables carried messages in the air or under the sea, dispensing with human messengers, the telegraph stations were still located on land that was under the jurisdiction of either established or emerging nation-states.

In most countries of Europe, the telegraph became the property of the state. When international agreements were made about the telegraph at the conferences of representatives of government telegraph departments and companies held in Paris in 1865, Vienna in 1868, Rome in 1871 and 1878, St Petersburg in 1875, London in 1879, Berlin in 1885, Paris in 1890, Budapest in 1896 and London in 1903 (*Encyclopaedia Britannica* 1911b, 529), the arrangements acknowledged that the lines were national property. The conferences defined collaboration between telegraph companies located in different countries in accordance with the legislation of those countries. The conferences acknowledged the power of nation-states and agreed on international co-operation for the transmission of messages across borders. The telegraph (news) agencies simply adopted this policy, although they also expanded their activities beyond the countries in which they were located.

London was the capital not only of the United Kingdom, but also of the whole British Empire. Potter writes

> The late 19th century saw the emergence of an embryonic imperial press system, composed of complex commercial links between private press enterprises around the British world. Crucially, the emergence of London as a centre from which the rest of the British world drew its news helped ensure that papers in each of the Dominions would continue to share the same basic perspectives on international events, even if editorial opinions varies. (Potter 2003, 212)

Greenwich, near London, became the location of zero longitude in a worldwide reckoning system. The Paris observatory served a similar, alternative, function. In 1884, the International Meridian Conference voted to make Greenwich Time valid for the whole world (Rifkin 1987, 144–145). The acknowledgement of the power of nation-states also acknowledged the power of new electronic empires. London was the capital of the UK and also became the capital of the electronic empire since most cables and messages crossed London. By 1902, with the construction of the Australian cable, the UK was in control of a cable ring around the world (Höhne 1977, 37). By 1907, more than 38,000 nautical miles of submarine cables had been laid, mostly under British ownership and control. With the outbreak of World War I in 1914, practically all cable lines led to London (*The Radio Industry* 1928, 71).

The expansion of cable strengthened the position of London as a communications hub of the world. Reuters was now able to establish its own electronic network around the world It was a very hierarchical network, where London had power over other cities. The scheme which Sir Roderick Jones, Reuters' General Manager, presented in the late 1920s as the organization's overseas structure exemplifies this global network structure,with London as the hub connected to other regional hubs via the telegraph:

> Each general manager is responsible to the head Administration in *London* for the Managers, Agents and Correspondents within his territory.
>
> *Shanghai's* jurisdiction extends from the Straits, north and east, over China, Manchuria, Siberia, Korea, Japan, the Philippines, Borneo, and the Dutch East Indies.
>
> *Bombay* has jurisdiction over India, Burma, Ceylon, Siam, Tibet, Afghanistan, Persia, Mesopotamia and Turkestan.
>
> *Cairo* is responsible for Egypt, the Sudan, Abyssinia, Palestine and Arabia.
>
> *Melbourne's* authority covers Australia, New Zealand and the Pacific islands.
>
> *Cape town* is responsible for the Union of South Africa, South West Africa, Portuguese East Africa and Rhodesia, beyond the Zambezi and up to the Great Lakes.
>
> *New York* has charge of the R staff and operations in the USA, South America and Ottawa similarly in Canada.
>
> The Continent of Europe, from Helsingfors [Helsinki] to Madrid, and from Christiania to Constantinople, comes directly under the head Administration in *London*, as do also East and West and Central Africa, South America, and other territories not included in one or other of the Seven general managerships.[2]

The structure reveals two interesting distinctions. First, regional hubs were not necessarily the capitals of their respective countries, but commercial centers that were connected to each other via the telegraph and submarine cables. Second, they served as centers not only for the countries they were located in or even for their neighboring countries, but also for countries that were connected to each other through technology. The telegraph created a new mental map where older political and cultural differences were overlooked and countries were bundled together almost arbitrarily. Here we see the origins of the first global electronic network society based on the telegraph. However, this new network structure which overlooked national boundaries was to be challenged by the *nationalization* of news.

Thus London became the news capital of the world. It was to maintain this position until New York rose to challenge it. As US officials testified in 1919:

> There is no question that London is the cable center of the world. Being the cable center of the world, it is the news center of the world, and part of the British position throughout the world is due to the fact that London is the great center for distribution of news. (Rogers 1919b, 110)

London's central position is also shown in actual news. Traditionally, news flows studies (for example Sreberny-Mohammadi et al. 1985) have shown from which *nation-states* news came. However, if one looks more closely, one sees that most news actually came from the cities, not from the nation-states. Nation-states are not equally covered by news flows; news comes rather from a few cities There are very few news studies that have not used the nation-state as their starting point, but the few that are available confirm the dominant position of these cities.

One of these studies is that of Wilke from 1984. He compared the number of news stories coming from different European cities between 1622 and 1906. His research shows the position of certain cities, but also the change in their status that supports Braudel's theory of domination and decline.

Another study, of Russian newspapers, shows that in the nineteenth century, for example, from the time the first electronic news was published in 1856, London was the leading news center, followed by Paris, Berlin, and Vienna, with two thirds of electronic news emanating from these cities. When there was a war, the percentage dropped and news starting coming from battle fronts, but the cities regained their pre-eminence once the crisis had passed. Even at the beginning of the twentieth century, almost half of all telegrams published in Russian newspapers came from the four cities of London, Paris, Berlin, and Vienna. Furthermore, all four leading cities began to operate as transmission centers, funneling news from other cities. A closer analysis revealed that a high percentage of London telegrams came originally from New York, Bombay, or Shanghai (Rantanen 1990, 145–166).

Table 2.3 The ten most important news cities for German newspapers between 1622 and 1856

1622			1674	
Prague	15.6		Strasburg	10.4
Vienna	12.4		Warsaw	9.4
Haag	8.9		Niederelbe	8.9
Frankfurt	7.6		Vienna	6.2
Cologne	6.2		Antwerpen	5.7
Venice	5.3		Haag	5.5
Amsterdam	5.1		Venice	4.7
Regensburg	4.4		Amsterdam	4.2
Rome	4.1		Copenhagen	3.4
Bünden	<u>3.0</u>		Paris	<u>3.4</u>
	72.6			61.8

1736			1796	
Paris	16.0		Paris	26.6
Vienna	12.0		London	11.7
London	9.9		Vienna	9.1
Haag	6.3		Haag	5.4
Copenhagen	5.9		Frankfurt	5.4
St Petersburg	3.6		Copenhagen	4.3
Naples	3.2		Stockholm	4.3
Warsaw	3.1		Italy	3.5
Dresden	2.7		Main	3.3
Rome	<u>2.7</u>		Mailand	<u>2.8</u>
	65.6			76.4

1856	
London	11.8
Paris	10.8
Hamburg	8.6
Berlin	7.4
Madrid	7.2
St Petersburg	5.2
Vienna	5.1
Constantinople	4.2
Vienna	1.8
Frankfurt	2.6
Naples	<u>2.6</u>
	68.4

Source: Wilke 1984, 251.

Table 2.4 The main transmission centers of foreign telegrams in Russian news-papers in 1870 (%)

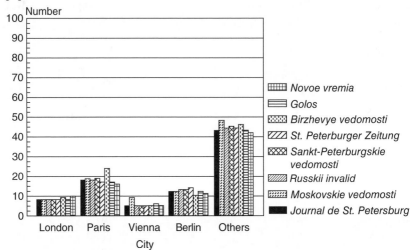

Source: Rantanen 1990, 155.

Beyond the Nation-state: City to City

The history of media and communications has mainly been a narrative of nations and relations between nations. This is a useful approach, but also limits our understanding. The narrative easily becomes repetitive and prevents researchers from seeing networks that cross the boundaries of nation-states. This is especially true with the pre-telegraph networks that were primarily based on the exchange of news between cities, not all of which were capitals.

Even early telegraph news crossed the boundaries of nation-states effortlessly. The founders of the first telegraph agencies themselves based their business on the exchange of news between cities in different countries. This was the traditional way: political and financial news flowed between major cities in Europe. The exchange of news was vital for the status of these cities as centers. The most networked cities were also the most influential: using Braudel's term, they were world cities.

In these cities, people's nationality or religion was not the most important dividing factors; there were others, such as wealth, gender, or ethnicity. Many world cities contained many worlds inside them, because they attracted people from other places to live and work there. There was a certain degree of messiness and, as a result, a toleration of differences. These cities had a life, a world, of their own and looked for inspiration to other cities, not to the countryside. A city way of life was distinctively different from life in the country.

One of the key differences was connectivity. Connectivity is not just transportation, but transmission. In the pre-telegraph era these two went together: a message had to be transported either by foot or by carriage. As a result, there was "in-between" time, between the departure and the arrival of a message. But this did not mean that cities were not widely connected – they indeed had world-wide connections. The telegraph changed this, because news could now be transmitted instantaneously. A new product was born: telegraph news, which combined content (news) with technology. News, of course, was "invented" long before the telegraph, but it was this combination that made news new.

Electronic news was a child of cities where both technology and content producers were present at the same time. Castells writes of how a global city epitomizes the contradictory logic of the space of flows. He writes

> While reaching out to the whole planet second by second and round the clock, it relies on the spatial proximity of its different command centers, and on face-to-face interaction of its anonymous masters. Based on telecommunications and information systems that overcome time and distance, it needs a technological infrastructure that can only be provided by the agglomeration of economies and access to scarce skilled labor. (Castells 1989, 344)

The technological infrastructure for the production of electronic news was already present in cities in the nineteenth century. Castells (1989, 13) also writes that the new information-based production is characterized by two fundamental features. First, the new technologies are focused on information processing. The real change, compared to an industrial form of production, is that information is both the raw material and the outcome. Second, the major effects of technological innovations are on processes, rather than on products. Again we see that the outcome had already changed with the advent of telegraph news and that we are also talking here about the early forms of information goods.

When the telegraph was introduced in Europe in the first half of the nineteenth century, new information cities – later to become global cities – emerged, based on the early form of telecommunications. Berlin, Paris, and London became the most connected cities in Europe – connected first with each other and then as hubs for the rest of the world. But it was not only technology that connected them, since they also became, with the foundation of the first telegraph and later the news agencies of Havas, Wolff, and Reuter, centers for information providers. Ahead of their time, the early news agencies operated first not as national agencies, but to provide news to their clients in their home cities and other cities in Europe; only later did they become national agencies.

Introducing cities as a starting point for analysis opens up new ways of understanding empirical materials that were previously theorized using the national–international framework. Telegraph agencies, as the first global providers of electronic news, have traditionally been divided into two categories: international and national. This division, although it helped in understanding some aspects of their operations, prevented us from seeing that the research was missing other important aspects. Careful study of the early history of telegraph agencies in the nineteenth century reveals in fact that the nationalization of news was an outcome of their development rather than a reason for it, since the first agencies operated primarily for clients in the cities where they were located and first established contacts with other cities outside their home countries.

The difference between electronic and pre-electronic news was that in most European countries the telegraph became government-owned and -controlled. It was in the interest of governments to use it as a medium primarily for nation-states. Subsequently, the telegraph became international, connecting nation-states, because government representatives made decisions about its interstate use. Even if Messrs Havas, Wolff, and Reuter had wanted to continue their operations as an intercity activity, they would have been going against the tide of nationalism.

The second coming of the global cities is of course the globalized Information Age. As Sassen (1994/2006, 6) writes, including global cities in our analysis adds three important dimensions to it. First, it breaks down the nation-state into a variety of components. Second, it displaces our focus from the power of large corporations over governments and economies to the range of activities and organizational arrangements necessary for the implementation and maintenance of a global network of factories and markets. Third, it contributes to a focus on place and on the urban social political order associated with these activities. In short, the latest media and communication technology in global cities makes holes in the national boundaries tightened in the Industrial Age. Sassen (2004, 651) writes that the new network technologies, especially the Internet, have ironically strengthened the urban map of these transboundary networks. She writes

> In so doing these technologies can also help the formation of cross-border public spheres for these types of actors and can do so (1) without the necessity of running through global institutions, and (2) through forms of recognition that do not depend on much direct interaction and joint action on the ground. (Sassen 2004, 654)

In relation to news this means that organizations, individuals, and the media themselves are less dependent on national newsgatherers but instead can rely on their own intra- and inter-city digital networks. Thus, for example, in its original sense, an individual citizen (*civitas* in Latin meaning city), as an inhabitant of a particular city, does not any more need to go to news provided by a national news organization but instead can go directly to a medium in another city through the Internet.

The use of private digital networks is easy to observe in many instances, including financial firms and diasporic groups in cosmopolitan cities when they use media and communications beyond their location. In this way, a transnational company is less and less dependent on national/state networks. Or a British Pakistani in London does not necessarily watch the BBC news but instead goes to the website of *Daily Pakistan* in Lahore or to *Pakistan Link* in Los Angeles. This does not mean that they are completely free of their nation-states they are located in. But it re-emphasizes again the importance of cities for any analysis of news, either historical or contemporary.

Notes

1 www.thurnundtaxis.de/frs_home.html, accessed October 27, 2008.
2 Sir Roderick Jones papers. A note on Reuters. For private information only. Printed by Waterlow and Sons Limited, London, Dunstable, and Watford. Reuters' archive, box file 97.

3

Globalization

When News Became Global

In an age of intrusive electronic communication "now" becomes an extended interval of time that could, indeed must, include events around the world. (Kern 1983, 314)

News organizations are probably the most invisible of all media organizations. Since in the past they often operated as retailers selling news to other media, their significance is often neglected. They are very much part of the professionalization of news in the nineteenth century when news became a global good. As a matter of fact, electronic media, including news organizations, would appear to be excellent examples of the modern organizations which Giddens said "are able to connect the local and the global in ways which would have been unthinkable in more traditional societies and in doing so routinely affect the lives of many millions of people" (Giddens 1990, 20).

Paradoxically, the important role that news organizations have played in the history of globalization has been simultaneously acknowledged and disregarded in the works of globalization theorists. Most globalization theorists refer to the role of mass media in the process of globalization while simultaneously ignoring them in at least two different ways. First, they are mainly interested in the present and ignore the history of cultural globalization. Second, as a result of this their main emphasis has been on the globalized role of modern media, that is, television.

Obviously, as Giddens writes, the global extension of the institutions of modernity would be impossible if not for the pooling of knowledge which is represented by the "news" (Giddens 1990, 77–8). News agencies were the first electronic mass media organizations to start operating globally in the first half of the nineteenth century. The fact that scholars outside communication research have nonetheless been able almost completely to ignore them is probably due to the invisibility of the historical development of news agencies even to communication scholars.

Only in the 1970s did we see a brief explosion of news agency studies. Boyd-Barrett (1986, 69) divides the research on news agencies into in terms of three major approaches: (1) analysis of content; (2) studies of structure and function; and (3) historical accounts of agency development. Each of these approaches has contributed something to the study of globalization, but none is completely satisfactory for the purpose of this chapter. The first category of study, analysis of content, has its origins in the early 1950s (*The Flow of News* 1953) and can be labeled as news flow studies. These studies demonstrated that the overwhelming majority of world news flows from the North to the South and from the West to the East. This news was generated by four big global agencies, the British Reuters, the US AP and UPI and the French AFP. Such concepts as imbalance and dependency were frequently used to describe the relationship between global and national agencies (MacBride 1980, 34–43).

The second category, research on structure and function, could largely be located within the tradition of a political economy of the media. As Garnham (1994, 6) writes, a political economy of communications and culture stresses that all mediated forms of communication involve the use of scarce material resources: that the understanding we have of the world, and thus of our ability to change it, will in turn be determined by the ways in which access to and control over those scarce resources are structured. Most of the studies of the political economy of the news agencies concentrated on their ownership and economics. These were sometimes combined with content analysis of the news delivered by the agencies (for example Harris 1977).

The third category of study, focusing on the historical development of news agencies, has its roots in the early twentieth century and has consisted mainly of a significant number of organizational histories of single companies. One of the few comprehensive scholarly studies of the global news system of the nineteenth century is Gunilla Ingmar's dissertation of 1973. Ingmar's work was the first scholarly study of the agreements made between the news agencies in the nineteenth century, and also focuses on the role of national governments in the formation of the global news system. A-historicism is a particularly striking and regrettable feature of much social science research, and this tradition has therefore contributed an important historical dimension to news agency research.

Each of the three traditions of news agency research I have presented has, of course, its own strengths in analyzing the process of globalization, but they have also neglected some important aspects. The news flow studies tradition lacks coherent theoretical concepts and has concentrated on the content of news. Studies of the political economy of the media have concentrated mainly on the contemporary conditions of production and the broader political and economic structures of society. The historical tradition of news agency studies have mainly focused on single companies.

Further, as Schlesinger (1995, 5–6) has observed, media histories in general have an overarching interest in showing how media institutions contribute to the shaping of a national culture, economy, and polity. There has been a growing recognition of the transnational, even global, framework as relevant for media analysis. Unfortunately, however, media histories have hardly touched on the global aspects of media development.

None of the above is a completely satisfactory approach to a historical perspective on news agencies and the process of globalization. What is needed is to overcome the exclusive disciplinary lines that have separated the different news agency research traditions. As I have pointed out in my earlier work, for example, the segregation of news agency studies into two discrete fields – international communication and journalism history – has led to misinterpretations of news agency operations (Rantanen 1992, 3). It is impossible to study news agencies, as global media organizations which sell news not only to every kind of media, but also to business enterprises, banks, and governments, without crossing disciplinary boundaries. They cannot be understood in terms only of the contents of news, of political economy or of institutional histories. What is needed in order to understand their complex nature is a holistic approach, at the crossroads of different existing approaches, placing news agencies in the context of the different elements of globalization such as commodification, national and international formation, time, space, and place. None of the approaches presented here has been able to combine these elements, although all have a contribution to make to an understanding of how news was turned into an object of global trade.

News as Business

People, whenever they gather, have always exchanged news. Stephens (1988, 25) writes that a symbiotic relationship between news and trade was established at the market place. News helps the merchants at the market to plan their strategies, and the goods that are being traded there attract people and therefore attract news. Hence, the connection between news and the market was created at a very early stage.

Benedict Anderson (1991, 34–5) writes that the book was the first modern-style, mass-produced industrial commodity. Anderson argues that books can be compared to other early industrial products, such as textiles, bricks or sugar, that are measured in mathematical amounts such as pounds or loads or pieces. According to him, the book, however – and here it prefigures the durables of our time – is a distinct, self-contained object, reproduced exactly on a large scale. Anderson says that the newspaper is merely an "extreme form" of the book, a book sold on a colossal scale, but of ephemeral popularity.

The nineteenth century witnessed the commercialization of news. As Baldasty (1992, 8) notes, previously partisan editors viewed their readers as voters. By the end of the century, editors and publishers saw their readers not only as voters but also as consumers. A *modern* newspaper was born in many countries by the latter half of the nineteenth century. Groth (1928, 22) defined a *universal* newspaper as one that: (1) is published regularly; (2) is printed mechanically; (3) is available to the public; (4) has comprehensive and universal contents; (5) has contents of general importance; (6) has current information; and (7) operates as an economic enterprise. Habermas (1989, 181–5) writes that the history of the big daily papers in the second half of the nineteenth century proves that the press itself became manipulative to the extent that it became *commercialized.* In consequence, the relationship between publisher and editor changed. Editorial activity had, under the pressure of the technically advanced transmission of news, become specialized; once a literary activity, it had become a journalistic one (Baldasty 1992, 8). Schudson (1978, 4–5) writes that, until the 1830s, a newspaper provided a service to political parties and men of commerce; with the *penny press* a newspaper sold a product to a general readership and sold the readership to advertisers. The product sold to readers was "news."

Although the commercialization of news took place simultaneously in several countries, researchers have neglected the role of *news agencies* in the process of transforming news into a global commodity that was bought and sold on a mass scale. For example, Habermas (1989, 187) refers to the homogenization of news services by monopolistically organized press agencies, but pays no further attention to them. Schudson

(1978, 5) first admits that the emergence of the Associated Press was an obvious explanation of why the idea of news, once established, was turned into "nonpartisan, strictly factual news." However, he later rejects the explanation. The important question here is not whether news became more objective than it was before. I agree with those researchers who consider news as a social construct rather than an undistorted reflection of what occurs in the world (Baldasty 1992, 8). The distinction is crucial for the purposes of this chapter. As Baldasty (1992, 8) writes, news became a manufactured product in the nineteenth century, reflecting the requirements of the parties involved in its production, distribution, and consumption process.

In the nineteenth century not only newspapers, but also news became an industrial product, that similar in many respects to the book. The commercialization of news meant, among other things, that news became more important for newspapers, thus occupying more columns than ever before. However, news was different from the book in one respect: it was not durable. News received its value because of an opposite quality: because it was non-durable and consumed instantly.

Newspapers became ephemeral because news became ephemeral. The modern, universal, commercial newspaper needed news and competed for the latest news. First, it came out several times a week, later daily, and thus demanded much more news than its predecessors. It was news agencies that started the global mass-production of news and sold news to newspapers that in turn served it to consumers. As Palmer (1976, 206) writes, no newspaper could cover all categories of information – political, financial, and foreign – as completely, rapidly, and reliably as news agencies. News agencies became the wholesalers of news for banks, merchants, government circles and newspapers. The earliest news agencies were founded from the 1830s onwards. Once the first news agency was founded, that model was emulated by numerous followers in different countries. The most developed countries in Europe had news agencies by the 1870s. This coincides with the birth of the universal newspaper.

The study of news agencies is essential, if we want to understand how news was transformed into a commodity. At this point we need to ask questions. How did news agencies turn news into a commodity? What were the specific requirements for news to become an object of trade? What was changed when the first news agencies were founded? Here we come to the concepts of time and space that have been missing in the earlier traditions of news agency research.

News and Time

Most scholars admit that electronic media have changed the significance of space, time, and physical barriers as communications variables (Meyrowitz 1985, 13). According to Harvey (1989, 241), the objectification of space and time allowed time to annihilate space. He calls this process time–space compression, a development in which time can be reorganized in such a way as to reduce the constraints of space and vice versa. Giddens (1990, 19) writes that coordination across time is the basis of the control of space. Hence, time and space are inseparable. He writes

> The advent of modernity increasingly tears space away from place by foster-ing relations between "absent" others, locationally distant from any given sit-uation of face-to-face interaction. In conditions of modernity, place becomes increasingly *phantasmagoric*: that is to say, locales are thoroughly penetrated by and shaped in terms of social influences quite distant from them.

The fundamental change in the relationship between time and space coin-cides with the shift from printed to electronic culture. The telegraph, as the new technology that made electronic culture possible, has received the most attention. Carey (1989, 203), for example, considers the telegraph a watershed in communication. Among other things, it changed the nature of language, of ordinary knowledge, of the very structures of awareness. According to Meyrowitz (1985, 13), with the invention and use of the telegraph, the informational differences between different places began to erode and destroyed the speciality of place and time.

The close connection between news and time was developed in the nineteenth century. Of course, news has always been new, that is, something that was not available before. But before the invention of the telegraph, news always needed a carrier. News traveled as fast as its carrier did. As a result of the progress in transportation, major changes took place in time–space compression, namely the shrinking of distance in terms of the time taken to move from one location to another (Meyrowitz 1985, 116). For example, the journey from the East coast to the West coast of the USA took two years by foot, four months by stagecoach, but only four days by train (Lash and Urry 1994, 229).

It was the telegraph that separated a message from its carrier and con-nected news and time even more closely together. The use of the telegraph signal also made it possible to synchronize local time with Greenwich time.

The first international agreement was concluded in 1884 on the standard-ization of time zones (Lowe 1982, 37–8). The telegraph profoundly changed the relationship between news and time, because the value of news could be measured against time that had become quantified.

News agency histories provide several examples of how speed became all important with the use of the telegraph in news transmission Earlier, before the telegraph, news could be quite dated. In the beginning of the eighteenth century, the minimum transmission time from England to Mas-sachusetts was 48 days. The unofficial news about the death of King William in 1702 did not reach his American subjects until almost three months later (Stephens 1988, 220). New agencies, with the help of the telegraph, changed weeks into hours.

Hence, with the telegraph, speed became a key feature in the commodity exclusivity nature of news. Bücher (1908, 227) defined news as a product that is valuable as long as it is recent. Elliot and Golding (1974, 248) write about the concept of commodity exclusivity that is based on two features of the production process – speed and originality. They write

> In industry, where competition for markets and competition within markets is an increasing pressure on the organization, speed has become one of the major tenets of news-media organizations. It is imperative to supply markets ahead of competitors. The necessity of gathering, processing, and distribut-ing information as quickly as possible has implications for the type of com-modity produced.

News agencies became large-scale users of the telegraph. Although the first agencies that were founded before the telegraph still had to rely on mail or pigeons, they adopted the new communication technology as soon as it was available for use. If readers consumed newspapers at daily or half-daily intervals, newspapers began to consume news from news agencies at even shorter intervals. With the help of the telegraph, news agencies could provide telegrams not just daily, but every hour, and in due course every minute and second. The instant flow of news was first created by news agencies in the nineteenth century and only later in this century adopted by the electronic media. News agencies could have provided news directly to readers in the way they provided it to their clients in business and in government. In the nineteenth century, however, consumers' time had not been filled with news in the way, for example, that CNN fills the day today. And here we come to the question of space, which is so closely connected with time that it is impossible to separate the two.

News and Place

As I pointed out earlier, as long as people gathered at the market places to exchange news, news was connected with places. News could be old or even have come from distant places, but it was people who exchanged it. Most news was about places that people knew about. Hence, the exchange of news was a social relationship based on face-to-face communication, taking place in a community context and connected to place.

It is also important to note at this point the close connection between place and news. According to Sack (1992, 2), place and consumption are connected for the obvious reason that we must consume things in place, that consumption takes place in a locality. Most news delivered at market places had an obvious connection with the lives of those people who delivered and received it in their localities. Place, unlike space, is something familiar, authentic and concrete ("there is no *place* like home") (Relph 1976, 63–78). News was local in that it was connected with the daily life of the places in which people lived.

Augé (1995, 82) writes that the term space is more abstract in itself than the term place, whose usage often evokes a particular event which has taken place. When news began to be delivered from remote places by mass media, it began to lose its immediate connection with people's ordinary lives. As Schivelbusch (1978, 37) notes, only when modern transportation creates a definite spatial distance between place of production and place of consumption do commodities become homeless. Within the spatial distance that the product covers on its way from its place of production to the market, he writes, it also loses its local identity, its here-and-nowness.

The use of the telegraph gave news an intrinsic connection not only with time but with space. Whilst transmitting news in the same way that other commodities were transported by train or ship, it was also revolutionary in conveying it without a carrier and at the instantaneous speed of electricity.

Electronic news differed from other kinds of products in two respects. First, it no longer needed a carrier. Second, it was not transported in large quantities like bricks or corn. Rather, a single news dispatch could be sent by the telegraph simultaneously to different points around the world, where it was duplicated by news agencies in their news bulletins for their clients. The telegraph, then, was the crucial technology, but it was news agencies which made telegrams into a mass media product, news.

Thus, the exchange of news first became a *mediated interaction*. Thompson labels this new type of relationship as mediated *quasi*-interaction (Thompson 1995, 84), since the news that had earlier been exchanged by people in a face-to-face relationship was now transmitted by the media. The word "quasi," however, can denote "as it were," "almost," "virtually," "rare," giving a connotation of being less real. This, I would emphasize, was a new kind of social relationship that did not replace face-to-face contacts, but gave rise to mediation as a key concept. The same news was now for the first time received by people who did not know each other personally, but who were in connected with each other through a *mass mediated social relationship* (Harvey 1993, 14). The place of news exchange, where people knew each other, became an abstract electronic space held together by mass media. As Thompson (1994, 35–6) writes, mediated quasi-interaction is monological in character, in the sense that the flow of communication is predominantly one-way. However, if we understand "quasi" primarily as "as if it were," we can understand this new type of relationship as still a *social* relationship even if no longer face-to-face.

This is also the point at which local markets turn into national markets, which then turn into global markets. When news was sent from one country to another, it crossed national boundaries and became universal because it could be used everywhere. s In every country where dispatches were received, news agencies translated these into the national language and, after reviewing and editing, transmitted them to their clients. Thus every agency operated in a double role on global markets: as a distributor of their own national news and as a receiver of global news. The junctures and disjunctures between global and national are also found in this relationship.

European countries were connected by the telegraph in the 1850s, but the oceans still separated continents. This obstacle was first overcome in 1851, when a submarine cable was laid between Calais and Dover. Ten years later, Europe and America were connected by an undersea cable, and this was followed by cables linking Africa and India in the 1860s, and China, South America and Japan in the 1870s.

Thus the new telegraph technology created instant connections between continents which earlier had been in touch on an irregular basis and with long delays in time. It should be remembered, however, that these connections were limited to the largest centers, capitals or major industrial cities. The three pre-eminent European news agencies – Havas in France, Reuters in Britain and Wolff (CTC) in Germany – became global agencies in the first years of their operation, while other agencies continued to operate within a national framework. The distinction is fundamental: national agencies operated inside the territory of their home countries, whereas global agencies expanded abroad. Coincidentally, France, Britain, and Germany were the countries with extensive telegraph nets: 89.6 percent of the world's telegraph cables belonged in 1892 to private companies (of which 63.1 percent were British). The British and French Empires also possessed over 60 percent of all government-owned cables (Headrick 1991, 38–9).

Newspapers depended upon news agencies which, in turn, depended upon the extension of the telegraph net. As a result, news agencies followed the cables. Of course, Reuters, and Havas benefited most from their domestic-owned cables, but Wolff (CTC) also extended its operations to other continents. For example, Julius Reuter started his agency in London in 1851, one month before the opening of the Calais–Dover cable, the world's first undersea link. Following the progress of the cable, Reuters opened offices in Alexandria in 1865, Bombay in 1866, Melbourne and Sydney in 1874 and Cape Town in 1876. Reuters was the only agency to finance telegraph cables: Julius Reuter's motto was "follow the cable" (Read 1994, 202).

Elliot and Golding (1974, 248) write that the concept of commodity exclusivity is based on two related features of the production process – speed and originality. According to them, the latter has important implications for the news-media production process; just as in the manufacturing industries the originality of a commodity is a source of advantage in the atmosphere of competition, so too in news-media organizations the originality of a news story provides advantages. It is the aim of every news-media organization to supply the subscriber with a news story which rival news media are unable to provide.

Traditionally, originality has been connected only with the contents of a news story – that means a story about a previously unknown event. But there is another factor that has been neglected by previous research: the place. News flow studies have in fact indirectly touched the problem by coding the origins of news. Unfortunately, they have concentrated on nation-states (examining, for example, what percentage of news originates in the USA, see Sreberny-Mohammadi et al. 1985) rather than places as such. The concept of commodity exclusivity could also be extended to places.

Place is important in news because events take *place*. I would take as an example news transmission in Imperial Russia in the nineteenth century. The news bulletins provided by Russian agencies did not carry headlines and appeared in random order, separated only by an indication of the place

ELECTRIC NEWS.

———•———

The following Telegram was received at Mr. REUTER's Office, November 24th.

St. PETERSBURG, Wednesday Nov. 24th.

On Saturday the Emperor received in audience the new Swedish ambassador Baron W. de Carlsberg, and the Bishop of Montenegro, Nicanor.

The Turkish ambassador Riza Bey took his leave of the Emperor.

———

Printed at Mr. REUTER's Office
1, Royal Exchange Buildings, City

Figure 3.1 Electric news in 1858. Published courtesy of the Reuters Archive.

(not country) of transmission and the date (i.e. Turin December 10, 1866). Newspapers followed this practice and often published the news bulletins just as they were. As a result, the place and date became the most important and distinctive feature of each news telegram (Rantanen 1990, 149–50). Time and place became the new criteria for evaluating news.

Elliot and Golding do not further define the components of originality in news. In its simplest form, this is something competitors lack. News agencies in the nineteenth century were the first to create electronic globalization by transmitting news from remote places. It become important to deliver news faster than competitors could deliver it, not only from local places, but also from more distant places.

My examples are again from Imperial Russia. In the early days, for example, Russian newspapers often offered no telegrams, but merely the announcement that "Today we did not receive telegrams." Russian papers received telegrams from cities outside Europe, the most remote being Macao, Tangier, Hong Kong and New York, but news from these remained relatively sparse. Most telegrams came from the major transmission cities, such as London, Paris, Berlin, and Vienna. The fastest telegrams from New York (via the Atlantic cable) still required between one and three days for delivery. Gradually, the average transmission time dropped to one day. By the beginning of the twentieth century, the number of telegrams from the main European transmission cities had declined and new non-European transmission centers had emerged (Rantanen 1990, 143–65).

Meyrowitz (1985) writes that electronic media create communities with "no sense of place." However, study of the process of production reveals a sense of place becoming in the nineteenth century even more important in the production of electronic news than it was before. The fact that news was transmitted from remote places, thus overcoming the obstacles of space, created a new kind of originality in the commodity exclusivity of news. News agencies competed against each other in transmitting news from remote places as fast as possible. Places also became an object of trade.

The Commodification of Global Electronic Space

As previously noted, it was the news agencies that started the global exchange of news by overcoming the obstacles of time and place. When time and place were filled, the new electronic space was still unconquered. Sack (1992, 42) writes that when areas of space are controlled, territories are created. By the end of the nineteenth century, at the same time that the dominant world powers took over the vast "open" spaces of other continents, news became global. According to Carey (1989, 212), it was the cable and telegraph, backed by sea power, that turned colonialism into imperialism. News agencies followed the cable and telegraph. It is no coincidence then that the news agencies of the world powers were the first to start news delivery from other continents.

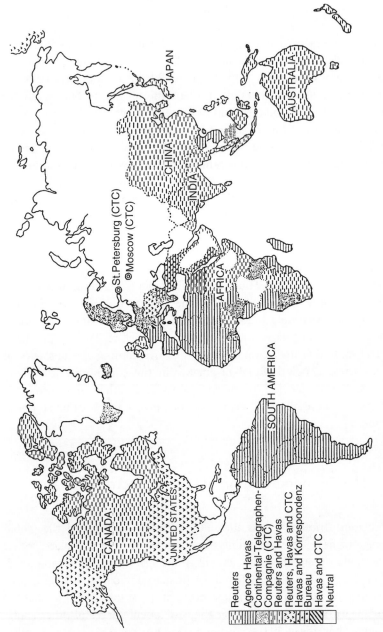

Figure 3.2 Territories of global agencies (1909 agreement) (Ingmar 1973, 24–25; in English, Rantanen 1990, 45).

As the world powers colonized vast territories of the globe, news agencies colonized their news by forming territories with restricted access. The first extant and verifiable agreement among the three global agencies – Havas, Reuters, and Wolff (CTC) – was signed in 1859. The agreements were amended and revised periodically and constituted the foundation of a powerful news cartel that divided up the world's news market among its members and lasted more than seven decades.

The central term, used as early as in the 1867 agreement between Havas, Reuters, and Wolff (CTC) and repeated in every agreement thereafter, was "exclusive exploitation" (*l'exploitation exclusive*) of news marketing in one's own territory. The agreements followed a set pattern: the global agencies received exclusive rights to the news for their territories. As Ingmar (1973, 28) writes, it was a sales monopoly: the party that controlled a territory had the exclusive right to the sale of news there.

The 1870 agreement gives some idea of how the cartel divided up the world's news market: it gave Reuters sole control over England, Holland, and their colonies; Wolff's share included Germany, Scandinavia, and the cities of St Petersburg and Moscow, and Havas received exclusive rights to France, Italy, Spain, and Portugal. The principle of exclusivity was later expanded into other territories as well. The 1874 agreement dealt not only with the old world, but embraced the entire globe (*concerne l'exploitation dans le monde entier*). The 1876 agreement between Havas and Reuters assigned South America to Havas, while India, China, and Japan were given to Reuters. By 1909 all the territories of the world had been divided up among Havas, Reuters and Wolff (CTC) together with the US Associated Press and the Austro-Hungarian Korrespondenz-Bureau as junior partners. The only undivided territories were Alaska, Russia (except Moscow and St Petersburg), Abyssinia, the Belgian Congo, Arabia, Afghanistan, Persia, and Siam (Rantanen 1990, 37–43). The national agencies simultaneously renounced their right to transmit news abroad, either directly or through any competing agency. Instead, they had to send and receive all their news through the global agency (or its counterparts) that had signed the agreement. The national agency also had to pay handsome commissions to the global agencies, not vice versa.

Hence, like time and place, electronic space also became not only commercialized but monopolized. Electronic space became territorialized; as Sack (1992, 83) writes, territoriality is a spatial strategy to make places instruments of power. News was no longer publicly exchanged in the open market, freely available for everyone to consume. It was treated as any other commodity and was even more carefully protected. Access to news sources, together with places, became restricted. By forming a news cartel, global news agencies significantly limited the competition by fixing prices, sharing markets and pooling profits. Coincidentally, the modern cartel movement in industry can be traced to the 1870s and 1880s when improved transportation, industrialization, and freer trade threw geographically insulated companies together with one another (Kahn 1968, 321). By colonizing electronic space, global news agencies monopolized news transmission in their exclusive territories and furthermore became prototypes for the global communications organizations to come.

The Global Electronic Space

According to Harvey (1989, 241), the major shrinking of the world map took place in 1850–1930 through innovations in transportation which annihilated space through time. This partly coincides with the second phase of globalization, in Europe, that Robertson (1992, 58–60) calls the incipient phase (1750–1875). Although Robertson mentions international communication only in the later context of what he calls the take-off phase (1875–1925), news agencies had already started operating earlier. News agencies played a major role in interconnecting places around the world and thus forming new global electronic space.

News agencies, with the help of the telegraph, were the first global media to initiate the distribution of electronic capabilities. They managed to overcome the geographical hindrances that had earlier prevented rapid news transmission from remote places. When news agencies began to use the telegraph, and especially submarine cables, they did something that had never been done before: created electronic news exchange between different places on a regular basis. Earlier, these places had been in touch with each other, but less frequently. Ships sailed between the continents, but there was always an element of unexpected delays that could be days, weeks or months long. In the new electronic age, the meanings of space and time changed.

This new global electronic space was produced by and based on a mass-mediated social relationship. Lefebvre (1991, 288) writes that spatial practices include the relationship of local to global. News agencies created electronically mediated relationship between places in different parts of the world. However, these places had different exchange values depending on their location and on transmission time (the time between the "event" and its reporting). Transmission time from a distant location had to be relatively short – from the leading transmission cities of the world, such as London, Paris, Berlin, and Vienna, it was, of course, even shorter. It is important to remember that, by interconnecting these places in global electronic space, the global news agencies set their own rules for the exchange of news. Whatever their geographical locations, cultural differences or technological capabilities, national news agencies had to be able to provide news about places inside their own national boundaries following the news time set by the global agencies, that is, to produce news regularly and quickly and following the universal news style. If they failed, they were perceived as not modern, labeled as underdeveloped or backward and were left out of the new global electronic space. Augé (1995, 77–8) uses the term non-place to describe places such as airports or shopping malls that are not relational, historical and concerned with identity. According to Relph (1976, 58), mass media produce mass-identities of places that are the most superficial identities of place, offering no scope for empathetic insideness and eroding existential insideness by destroying the bases for identity with place. In the global news flow, places can easily become phantasmagoric non-places, referred to only in the context of an event that has taken place there, and can lose their authentic local identity.

This leads us again to issues of inequality and dominance that are easily neglected when we talk about "abstract" things like time and space. For example, Morley and Robins (1995, 116) write of "global space, a space in which frontiers and boundaries have become permeable." In news agency research, both political economy and news flow traditions have underlined the concepts of inequality and dominance that should not be forgotten when discussing the new electronic global space of the nineteenth century. As the agreements between the international agencies indicate, when place and time were commodified in news, the electronic space did not remain open, but also became commodified. The globalization of electronic news, then, introduced its intensive commodification. Global space became a restricted space with frontiers and boundaries that were not permeable.

Note

1   http://dictionary.oed.com/cgi/entry/50194508?single=1&query_type=
    word&queryword=quasi&first=1&max_to_sh Accessed 10/27/2008/.

4

Commodification

How To Sell News

Sir Roderick [of Reuters] feels that it is a great pity that no one has ever effectively squashed the idea that it is immoral or something akin for a news agency to make profits out of selling news. One may make profits out of almost any other lines of business – alcohol, drugs, armaments, coffins, water, shelter, fiction – but NOT news. Why not? (W. Turner, Letter to Mr Moloney, May 23, 1935[1])

Thou shalt not steal news. (Mr Roigt, Fourth Plenary Meeting of the League of Nations Conference of Press Experts, August 25, 1927[2])

Why not sell news? How is it different from alcohol, drugs or water? And if you decide to sell it what makes it saleable? What are you buying when you buy news? Is it the "objectivity" of news, as both journalists and journalism scholars argue, that matters? Or is it the public's desire to learn the latest news?

Whenever news is studied, it is the content that attracts most attention. In this chapter, however, I want to focus on exploring the economics of news. When we turn our attention to the economics, the object of study changes: it is the institutions that produce the news which assume primary importance.

Equally, when seeking to investigate the economics of news, one needs to understand what news is. There is a lot of literature on news as a genre, but, again, this is not what this chapter is about. News as a genre, its format, is only interesting for my purposes as a "package," as something that separate news from other cultural goods. What we need to understand is *why* news needs a special format, a package that makes it into a good that can be sold and bought.

News Economy

Charles Havas, Bernard Wolff, and Julius Reuter, like the founders of today's dot.com companies, did something unprecedented and unthinkable: they combined the emerging technology of the early nineteenth century, the telegraph – the Internet of their time – with the idea of news as a wholesale business. And, as if this was not revolutionary enough, they started selling their new product, electronic news, not only nationally but globally, thus establishing business practices that have lasted until today and influenced every new global media industry organization that has been established since they started their companies. They started, in the age of industrialization, a new economic period – what Quah (2003) describes as the *weightless economy* – where the economic significance of *information* achieves its greatest contemporary resonance.

Nineteenth-century electronic news, compared to that of earlier times, was a new cultural good for its age. It differed, however, from other goods because it was rapidly turned into an exclusive good from which not everyone was able to benefit. To view it in this way is a very different approach from that of journalism studies which is most concerned about the content of such news, whether it is objective, whether it follows the best principles of journalistic writing. Here we are seeking to discover what made news into a weightless good that could be sold and bought on a mass scale.

A single news dispatch could be sent by telegraph simultaneously to different points in the world unlike heavy goods which would have to be transported separately in several directions. This new weightless information product, electronic news, could then be indefinitely multiplied around the world at little extra cost (such as translation if needed) and could be used by an indefinite number of customers (Rantanen 1997, 612).

The founders of the first telegraph agencies created this new kind of good by combining the old and the new: information with new technology, the telegraph. Hence, with the telegraph, speed became a key feature in turning news into goods that could be bought and sold. News became a property with specific characteristics, of which the most important was its novelty. As Bücher (1908, 227) wrote

> News is a good that is valuable as long at it is recent, and in order to retain the quality of freshness its publication must follow directly on the heels of the events themselves.

However, even if this new good could be defined as weightless, it was also heavy, sometimes even too heavy – heavy because it was a cultural good that, with the advent of the telegraph, started crossing cultural and national frontiers. News was heavy with content that could be shared in many places, but at the same time pregnant with contradictions. Everybody had an interest in news, not just individuals, but governments, companies, states, parties, and other organizations.

Private and Public Goods

Electronic news can also be conceptualized as cultural goods, in a similar way to other products of contemporary cultural industries. Cultural industries, since they produce content which can be shared, have usually been defined as institutions, most of which are directly involved in the production of social meaning (Hesmondhalgh 2002, 11). There are two kinds of cultural goods: private and public. Economic theory traditionally distinguishes between public and private goods. Public goods are defined as non-rivalrous because they can be used repeatedly, by many different users, in many different locations, without the original piece of information itself being degraded (Quah 2003). They are also non-exclusive, that is, once they have been created, it is impossible to prevent users from gaining access to them. There is also a third option: mixed (public and private) goods possess one of the characteristics of public goods, but not the other (non-rivalrousness or non-exclusivity) (Hoskins, McFadyen and Finn 2004, 295–296).

Electronic news was initially non-rivalrous, because it could be used by many different members of the audience, without their being in rivalry with one another. News could not be used repeatedly by the same individual, because news keeps its value only as long as it is new. It is thus a collective good that allows joint consumption when an additional user has no effect on costs (Hoskins, McFadyen and Finn 1997, 4) other than on that of transmission. Different users could make simultaneous use of news in different locations within different time zones. It was still new to them – even if users in other locations already knew about it, it had not been degraded.

This is why news has often been defined as a public good. However, news was also a private good, because it was created and sold by companies to their clients who were mostly not individual audience members, but other companies and institutions that had paid for their service and then re-sold or re-delivered it. News was rivalrous because they had paid for it and did not want to share it with others before they had used it. It became exclusive because every measure was taken to protect it. Once it had been delivered to its audience, it again became non-exclusive and non-rivalrous.

However, news as a public good was not what Havas, Wolff, and Reuter had in mind. On the contrary, when the transmission of electronic news started in the nineteenth century, what they did was to industrialize and commodify it. This process had already started with printing, when first charlatans and then newspapers started to sell new stories, but it reached a completely new level with the operation of telegraph agencies. Electronic news became a *private good*, rivalrous and exclusive, with clearly identified owners' companies that were named after their founders: Reuter, Havas, Wolff, etc. Telegraph agencies gathered and sold electronic news to their clients, which were firms, newspapers, and governments.

The founders of the first telegraph agencies changed information into news by gathering and processing it and then transmitting it to buyers. They considered it property because it cost them money and labor to produce it. Its values were its novelty, its accuracy and its presence in the place where there were enough interested clients to pay for receiving it at the time they wanted. The earliest telegraph agencies considered themselves organizations composed of capital and labor that created the commodity of news. The raw material was the information gathered, which was then turned into the final product of electronic news that was brought to the purchaser. In this way, telegraph agencies claimed that they created the product and thus owned the property rights to it.[3]

Electronic news lost its novelty, "went off," not in the same way, for example, as dairy products might, but because somebody else had already used it. Even if, as Quah (2003) argues, information products can be indefinitely expandable, electronic news loses its value and becomes non-expandable and degraded if one consumer uses it before others. Hence, on the one hand, electronic news is similar to other goods in that if one client receives it before others it can lose its value. On the other hand, if it is sent simultaneously to every client – be they companies, banks, newspapers, governments, or individuals- it does not lose its value, because many can use it at the same time.

Telegraphic news was innovative in the manner of its use: it could be used by many and in different ways. News can be new in two different ways, both of which contribute to its value as an object of trade. First, news is supposed to inform its recipients about something not previously known. This does not mean that it must have been completely unknown, but every piece of news has to add some information not previously known. Secondly – and increasingly so, but this was already true in the nineteenth century – news has to be recent in the sense that the time between the "event" the news is based on and the reception of the news has to be as short as possible. The telegraph contributed to this by compressing time and space. With the use of the telegraph news started to travel by itself and thus became new in a sense in which it never had been previously.

The clients of the early telegraphic news agencies needed to receive news early, preferably earlier than others, but after receiving it they could modify it, add information to it, and in the case of newspapers publish it. Telegraph news became a mass product because it was weightless and could easily be multiplied by the telegraph. Clients of telegraph agencies had to accept that they were all treated in a similar way: nobody could receive news faster than they did. The news dispatched by the agencies could be published as it was, as often happened in the early days, but newspapers could also use it as a raw material to turn into their own news, which then became theirs.

There are several weaknesses in the nature of the electronic goods created by telegraph agencies. First, there is a disagreement about the difference between information and news. Information was considered as a public good and thus non-rivalrous and non-exclusive. Although the early telegraph agencies acknowledged that there was no exclusive right to or monopoly on information, i.e., everybody had the right to gather information, they claimed that they had exclusive rights to their news, the good they had created from the information. Second, there was a disagreement about the length of their exclusive rights. By selling news to their clients, news agencies were in danger of losing those exclusive rights because it then became the property of the buyer who could do whatever they wanted with it, even sell it on to a third party. Third, when individuals bought newspapers, news became a public good to which everybody had a right. At every stage of the cycle of electronic news production, the exclusive nature of the new product was to be contested and eventually lost.

The early telegraph agencies tried to sell their news to as many clients as possible. Their original clients were banks, firms, private individuals and governments, but they soon started selling to newspapers as well. There was no reason to limit their activities to just one country: on the contrary, electronic news could be used in many locations if it was translated. The first European news agency proprietors were cosmopolitans of their time: they moved easily from one European city to another. Once they had established their respective bureaus in Paris, Berlin, and London they continued selling their news across borders. This was made possible by the telegraph, which compressed space and time and made location less important, even if the cost of transmission was higher.

In trying to solve the contradiction that is embedded in the nature of electronic news, the first electronic agency proprietors discovered early that they could sell their product outside their home market, i.e. their home country, to other markets where it could be re-sold, – in these locations it was still new since nobody else had used it. This is why electronic news became a global good at an early stage. By transmitting a piece of news with the help of the telegraph to another market, for example, from London to New York, they were able to re-sell it to another set of customers who were competing for the latest news. Hence, news became a transnational product that could be easily transmitted from one market to another. In doing this, telegraph agencies made sure that this key quality of news, its novelty, could be multiplied in different time zones.

Costs

The major costs of newsgathering can basically be divided into two categories: (1) transmission costs; (2) salaries. As we can see from Table 4.1,

Table 4.1 Budget for a worldwide news service

	Per annum $	%
Cable and wireless tolls	1,400,000	18
Leased wires and telegraph equipment	2,100,000	26
Local telephone and telegraph tolls	550,000	7
Mechanical and administrative payroll	900,000	11
News payroll	1,600,000	20
Part-time correspondents and tipsters	500,000	6
Taxes (federal, state and foreign countries)	200,000	3
Income taxes of American employees abroad	20,000	
Rents	250,000	
Travel	200,000	3
Supplies and stationery (including teletype paper)	250,000	
	7,970,000	

Source: Benét 1933, 98

different kinds of transmission costs make up 51 percent of the annual budget, while salaries make up 37 percent.

Companies

When it is cheaper to make transactions as an organization than as an individual, organizations will form (Seely Brown and Duguid 2002, 23). This premise may be applied to news production: whenever is cheaper to buy news than to produce it oneself, news agencies will form. When it is cheaper for an organization to produce news than it is for an individual (such as Messrs Havas, Reuter, and Wolff), organizations will form. News agencies were needed to do the job of gathering information and transforming it into news. Individuals or newspaper organizations could do that themselves, but the production costs were less when it was done by an agency that had access to information, to qualified workers to gather and edit the information, and to technology.

News agencies could also "pool" their resources by buying news from each other and thus saving in gathering and transmission costs. This is the reason why Havas, Reuter, and Wolff originally combined their resources: it made sense that one territory was not necessarily covered by all of them, but they relied on the exchange of news between them to provide their service to their clients. However, it was essential, they share the same news concept, that their product be standardized to an extent such that it could be recognized everywhere as news.

Technology

Technology affects news in at least five different ways. First, it gives news one of its vital components, its novelty. This is not just a matter of the time between the incidence of news and its publication, but also of news losing its value sooner than other cultural goods. Second, it allows news to be sold in different time zones, and thus to be sold several times in different markets. Third, technology enables the transmission of news about distant places as if they were close. Fourth, technology affects the pricing of news. Transmission costs have a direct effect on how news is priced.

This was especially important in the early days of the telegraph cables, when transmission costs were dependent on distance. Fifth, technology has an influence on the format of news. In the early days, news had to be as short as possible, in order to save on transmission costs. This created the so-called "telegram style" when news had to be worded as economically as possible.

News also needs two technologies for two types of circulation. Once the good, news, has been manufactured, it needs to be sent to its customers, newspapers. This is where the technology of the telegraph and wireless telegraph are used to *transmit* the news. The newspapers then "send" it to their audience by printing it and by *transporting* it to be sold or distributed directly to their subscribers. Unlike electronic goods in the information age, electronic news in the age of industrialization still needed to be both transmitted and transported. The combination of the two resulted in a delay compared with the instantaneous character of news that characterizes the age of information.

Format

News has to be recognizable as news, because this gives it a special status which other genres lack. It also needs to be distinguishable from information that is freely available. It has to follow a certain style (who says what, when, and where), because it is used transnationally. News has to be constructed in such way that it can be easily cut, pasted, and re-written, either wholly or partially, by different media in different parts of the world. This has also do to with so-called objectivity, which is not in fact about how objective news is, but how it represents different views so that it can be used by different media all over the world. Above all it has to be reliable, because this is how this particular cultural product is branded. It cannot falsify facts (falsely announcing the end of World War I), even if it can be partial (depending on whose viewpoints it represents).

Markets

Thanks to technology, news can be easily reproduced and transmitted to several clients simultaneously. This is a factor that leads to conflict, because everybody wants to have the news first, but not everybody can afford to have it first. When it is cheaper to gather, edit, and transmit news for individual clients, they do it themselves (for example, local news). When it becomes very expensive to do this, joint organizations are formed or news is bought from a supplier, i.e. a news agency. The news market is ultimately dependent, as is any market, on how much demand there is. When the market is saturated with news, only organizations that can produce different kinds of news (for example financial news) will survive.

News agencies have traditionally had a dual market, with two very different groups of customers. The first group consisted of individuals such as bankers, stockbrokers, and merchants whose primary interest was in financial information, and diplomats and courts who were interested in foreign news. Financial news was primarily financial information about prices on the stock market. The second group of customers was newspapers who wanted not only financial, but also political news. The possibility of having two very different groups of customers again shows how flexible a product news is: it can be used for multiple purposes and in multiple forms. The dual market has existed from the birth of news agencies and has also resulted in the foundation of financial news agencies such as Bloomberg or primarily financial news agencies such as Reuters, which nowadays calls itself an information agency.

Most media still have a national market, defined by the borders of a state; there is a niche for national news. News can thus have several national markets; it can be used several times in different markets because these are located in different time zones and because each national medium in a different location can add a national component or view to the news. This is the *inter-nationalization* of the market, in the original sense of the word. It is not in fact international, but a series of different national markets. But it means that every agency has several markets, domestic and foreign, and that the news can be used in all of them.

Price

The pricing of news is problematic due to its dual nature as both a public and a private good. News changes its character during the production process. It starts out public, because the information was in most cases free, although its timing may make a difference (first priority). When this information is changed into news it becomes exclusive, a private good. It remains a private good until its publication, when it again becomes public and ceases to be news and again becomes information.

Pricing also depends on competition. Many agencies used to have a monopoly and thus no competition in their domestic market. This monopolistic position was often justified by the need for news as a public good that every newspaper, and thus indirectly the public, could afford. For the same reason, news and news technology were subsidized in direct or indirect ways. If there was no monopoly, as in the US market, there were usually monopolistic arrangements that prevented free competition (for example, AP members were not allowed to buy news from other companies or sell their news to non-members of AP).

Exclusivity in News

When Messrs Havas, Reuter, and Wolff made their new business innovation, they probably had no idea how difficult it would be to protect the new informational good they had created. Electronic news has a much shorter life than other cultural products such as books or photographs. News has been described as a time-bound good that only has value as long as it is new (Bücher 1915, 17). It is the most perishable of commodities (Rings 1936, 11). Electronic news loses its value much faster than other cultural products – there is no such thing as yesterday's news.

There are several stages in the cycle where electronic news, according to its proprietors, needs protection. During this cycle news is bought and sold, changing owner, but every time it changes owner it also changes form. And the question of exclusivity must also be raised again. News is a chameleon that is constantly reshaped and transformed into something that does not necessarily bear a resemblance to its previous form.

Telegraph agencies tried to solve the issue of public and private property in various ways. One was to separate information from news. In principle, information can be defined as something that is public, i.e. available to everybody; it is never in practice that simple. The early telegraph and later the news agencies, defined events as information. They saw that everybody had free access to events, which were seen in terms of public information. They did not consider facts, before these had been ascertained, to be property, unless these were held for some special purpose confidentially.

However, when these facts had been discovered, and had promptly and as a result of effort and expense, been compiled and put into an appropriate form, and were thus of commercial value by reason of the speedy use that could be made of them before they became generally known, they were property (Rosewater 1930, 283. As the AP wrote in 1917,[4] exclusivity in news means not an exclusive right or monopoly to all announcements of that happening, but that an organization has the exclusive right to the property which it has itself created – i.e., its own message from the happening to those who seek to buy.

Another argument used was that of the labor invested by news agencies in turning information into property. Sir Roderick Jones of Reuters also agreed that there could be no property right in a news event, only in the transformation of information into property. Jones wrote:

> But as regarded the principle of human enterprise, human labor, and the expenditure of money – anybody would suggest for a single moment that the product ought not to be protected – principle of property right. [. . .] There could be no property right in a news event. The news event belonged to everybody. The property right must rest with the product of those who took the event and conveyed it in a certain form from one part of the world to another. That was where the labor and the cost and the enterprise were engaged, and it was the product of that enterprise and of that cost and labor which was to be protected.[5]

There were two points at which news was extremely vulnerable: when telegraph agencies sold it to their customers and when their customers published it. The first instance, when news agencies sold it to their customers, was easier to control by using other mechanisms defined in their agreements. The distribution system, the telegraph, also protected the product, because it was difficult to steal it *en route* since it moved without a carrier and at the speed of electricity. The telegraph also made it possible to send news only to previously defined recipients, thus securing its safe arrival only into the hands of clients who had paid for it.

The crucial question was again time, now the time after the publication of news. How soon after its publication does news lose its value and become information that is available to everybody? In Australia, for example, because evening newspapers were eager to publish telegrams from the morning papers, the copyright was often extended to 72 hours. Even this was not enough. Western Australia's attorney general argued in 1895 that

> At present . . . no newspaper is allowed to re-publish telegrams which have appeared in another newspaper, until seventy-two hours, or three days, have elapsed from their first publications by the newspaper that received them and pays for them. This provision, it appears, does not prevent some country newspapers from making use of the telegrams received by the metropolitan press, without paying for them or acknowledging them in any way. They simply pirate the telegrams, which are wired to them by correspondents, immediately upon their publication in the Perth newspapers, and they republish them in their ordinary issues when the three days' protection has expired. (Putnis 2002)

When the *Chicago Tribune* arranged with the London *Times* for exclusive use in the USA of its copyrighted articles on the Boer War, AP's London correspondent continued to buy *The Times* on the street each morning and to send a compendium of its contents to the New York office as part of the day's news consignment. The *Tribune*'s protest was ignored and its petition for an injunction and damages contested and denied "as the exclusive right of publication at the common law terminated with the publication in London, no protection then exists beyond that expressively given by the statute" (Rosewater 1930, 280).

As Putnis (2002) observes, in many countries, news was not given special protection in copyright legislation. This is not surprising because it is not the first instance of technology preceding legislation. There are two conflicting views here about the exclusivity of news. The first argument is that when news is published it becomes public property and no copyright can attach to it (Putnis 2002). This was the practice in the pre-telegraph era, when newspapers just copied their news from other papers. It did not matter whether news was re-used, because the paper that published it first had an advantageous position simply by having published it first. As a result, most foreign news in most newspapers in the pre-telegraphic era was simply "borrowed" from other newspapers, referencing the source in accordance with good journalist practice (for example, Rantanen 1990).

The second argument, the intellectual property rights in news, was to be discussed in many parliaments and professional conferences and disputed in court cases for years to come and all around the world. The new technology of that time, the telegraph, made the question of exclusivity more complicated, because messages were carried instantaneously and simultaneously to several places, crossing national borders. With electronic communication, the reproduction and transportation of news was easier than ever before, but for exactly the same reasons it was much more difficult to control.

The question of exclusive rights to news has much to do with the ownership of news. The *form* of ownership was once considered a key factor. When ownership was private, news was considered to be like any good that could be bought and sold. With state ownership, news belonged to the state and was thus "public"; making a profit was not the primary motivation. With co-operative ownership, news was shared with the members of the association, but not with non-members.

Although most news agencies, whatever their form of ownership, agreed that their news had be protected by copyright law, they disagreed fundamentally about the nature of news, whether it was a good that was primarily manufactured in order to make a profit for its owners or a good to be also shared collectively. These two stances were not necessarily completely opposite, but were also seen to complement each other. However, when this occurred, other measures were needed in order to protect its exclusivity.

The Monopolization of News: Global and Domestic

Surprisingly, the monopolization of news, which has traditionally been understood as having primarily to do with private or state monopolies, has been an issue in two of the major domestic markets of the world, the USA and Australia (Rantanen 1997), where there was a long tradition of co-operative agencies being accused of having a monopoly over the domestic news market. As Shmanske (1986, 55) has shown, there is nothing morally superior in the co-operative form of ownership: it is merely the way in which the US Associated Press(es) practiced price discrimination and restricted membership.

However, we cannot understand the monopolization of news if we separate foreign and domestic markets. When electronic news became commodified and monopolized in the global market, the same happened in the domestic market. The crucial link here is the transformation of news into an exclusive good, not only in the global market but also in the domestic market. Much earlier research has failed to understand that this process occurs simultaneously in both markets.

Doing the business of news globally increases its vulnerability. If the early telegraph agencies were to sell directly to individual newspapers, as they sometimes did, they could not protect the exclusivity of their product.

Since telegraph agencies were being established in different locations, Havas, Reuter, and Wolff developed a system for selling electronic news globally. Since there was no system of copyright, news agencies created for themselves a system of exchanging news across national borders. This system was later called an international news cartel, and was based on agreement between Havas, Reuter, and Wolff, on the one hand, and between these and other agencies, on the other.

The system operated on the principles of non-rivalry and non-exclusivity among themselves and of rivalry and exclusivity with other companies. Electronic news was first considered to be non-exclusive and non-rivalrous and to be exchanged freely between Havas, Reuter, and Wolff; and then came to be viewed as exclusive and rivalrous and to be sold to other parties. In order to regulate and control the global sale of electronic news, the three agencies regularly signed agreements both among themselves and between themselves and other parties. The first of these was signed in Paris in 1859 and the last in 1932. The contract signed by Reuters and AP in New York in 1934 ended their arrangement for the exclusive exploitation of global news.

Although Messrs Havas, Reuter, and Wolff all established their own private companies, the private ownership was contested from the beginning. The idea of a co-operative news agency was important (for example, Boyd-Barrett 1998; Boyd-Barrett and Rantanen 2001), because co-operative agencies provided domestic and international news to their customers at a lower price than that at which those customers could provide such news for themselves. This in turn reduced the cost of news provision to the public and contributed to the establishment of the well-informed public which is necessary for democracy. They also served a wide range of customers: the media (from print to electronic, from large to small, from provincial to metropolitan, political, state, economic, and financial institutions, and individuals), and provided news in a format that could be edited, supplemented, and re-used simultaneously in many countries, thus contributing not only to the globalization of news but to the global experience of the public around the world.

In many other countries, governments succeeded in taking over news transmission, often justifying their actions by reference to the public interest. These governments owned or controlled the news agencies, which often operated as national agencies with a monopoly over their own domestic market. Before World War I, Russia, Germany, Austro-Hungary, and many Balkan countries had government news agencies. These agencies, like the private and co-operative agencies, also had foreign clients who paid for their service. They were government-owned, government-controlled, government-subsidized or all of these, and often enjoyed special fees for news transmission by a government-owned telegraph company. Their privileged position made it very difficult for private or co-operative agencies to compete with them on a national or international level.

In Australia, as in many other countries, there were voices arguing that governments needed to take a leading role in the provision and dissemination of telegraph news by establishing publicly funded, freely available news services (Putnis, 2002). Various Australian governments flirted with the idea of government provision of key overseas news to the public, on the grounds that this was the only way to ensure the fair distribution of important information. As Putnis points out, they did not succeed in their endeavors because the interest of private property in news was a key imperative, secured through the vehicle of copyright law (Putnis 2002).

Domestic Monopoly

The co-operative model, in which newspapers jointly own a news agency, is based on the idea that no profits are made, but that news is being shared among the members. The world's first co-operative news organization was the US Associated Press, established in 1846 (Blondheim 1994, 55). Six New York City newspapers formed an organization in order to share the cost of collecting news by means of "news boats," which met incoming ships from Europe. Later, AP was organized under the corporation laws of the State of New York. It was a co-operative, non-profit-making corporation without shareholders or other commercial form of ownership. Its members were to be elected, originally by the affirmative vote of no fewer than four-fifths of all the members of the Corporation. Upon termination, however, all rights and privileges of individual members could cease (*News Agencies* 1953, 43). This model was enthusiastically exported to the rest of the world with the US expansion, first to South America after World War I and then to the rest of the world after World War II (Cooper 1942).

A formal arrangement for co-operative newsgathering was made in 1848, when six New York morning newspapers (the *Courier & Enquirer, Express, Herald, Journal of Commerce, Sun,* and *Tribune*) agreed to share the costs of wire news. More or less accidentally, this grouping came to be known as the Associated Press, or in later years the New York Associated Press (Rosewater 1930; Swindler 1946, 44). As Swindler (1946, 44) observes, it was obvious from the beginning that the newspapers that founded the association wanted to keep tight control of it. A later president of the association stated that "we do not propose to delegate any authority . . . News gathering is our business enterprise and we do not propose to share it with others" (Gramling 1940, 44; see also Stone 1921, 210–211).

The organization's formal regulations (Rosewater 1930, 381), from 1856, revised and strengthened the control of its members, stating that

1 All telegraphic news, with certain stated exceptions, was to be available to all members.
2 No new members were to be admitted without unanimous consent.
3 News obtained by the members or their agents might be sold to other parties for the general benefit of the Association.
4 No member newspaper should obtain news from any non-member newspaper, or other new association, or release news to it. (Swindler 1946, 44)

The idea behind a news co-operative is to share the costs of news production between the members. However, the protection of this good, which thus becomes public, but only public among the members, requires a concept of exclusivity, since, although it is a public good, it cannot be shared by those who have not paid for it. As Swindler (1946, 46) has pointed out, the new Associated Press of Illinois (founded in 1892) continued with a policy which was fundamentally that of the earlier associations:

1 Its by-laws provided for exclusive membership and no intercourse with other newspapers or news agencies.
2 No new members were to be accepted in areas where AP newspapers were already published, except in accordance with the by-laws of local members or their boards.
3 No member was to accept or furnish news to outsiders or to publish it in advance of the released date.

AP's domestic exclusivity policy invited several suits against it. As Swindler (1946, 47) writes, the *New York Sun* sued the AP in 1898 following the decision of other AP newspapers not to have dealings with it because of its "antagonism." The *Sun*'s pursuit of an injunction was denied and the civil suit was settled out of court, but the *Sun* used the Federal anti-monopoly legislation (Sherman law) of 1890 and an Illinois anti-boycott statute of 1891 to pursue allegations in equity that the AP was seeking "contract combination or conspiracy to *monopolize* the gathering and selling of news." Other papers also sued the AP after not being accepted into the organization or because commercial telegraph companies were not providing equal facilities for all press messages (Swindler 1946, 47).

Another law case appeared in 1915 when the *Chicago Inter Ocean* was suspended by the AP after exchanging news with the *New York Sun*, which had been previously declared antagonistic to the association. The *Inter Ocean* sought an injunction and damages, and pursued the case from the original court, where the actions of the association were upheld, though the intermediate appeal court, which also found for the AP, to the state supreme court (see, for example, Rosewater 1930, Swindler 1946, Blanchard 1987). In 1942, the Department of Justice compiled a civil suit against the AP in 1942, based on the Sherman Anti-Trust Act, on the grounds that its activities constituted a combination and conspiracy in restraint of trade and commerce in news, information, and intelligence among the several states in an attempt to monopolize a part of such trade and commerce, and a combination and conspiracy to monopolize the same (Blanchard 1987, Rantanen 1998, 25). All these lawsuits exemplified that news had become business but whether news should be treated as any other business became a source of disagreement.

The End of the News Economy?

The industrialization of news changed new stories into news that could be bought and sold on a mass-scale. The process included professionalization in which the roles of transmitters, content providers, editors, etc. were separated from each other. At the same time, news was given its distinctive content, form, and time span. The new modern product, news, was ready to be taken into global mass-markets.

News from the beginning was a difficult product to price. Although it could be sold to many, it was a light good that easily lost its value. It was also difficult to show what was so distinctive about news that made it different from other information products. What did one pay for in news: content, speed, reliability, brand, or status? The new organizations behind news, news agencies, gave it the status, regularity, and brand that made news not from anywhere but from a recognizable and thus reliable source.

When technology was big and controlled by the state or large corporations it was much easier to make news exclusive. With the development of the latest media and communications technologies it has become very easy to "steal" news en route. In the Middle Ages new stories were mostly shared stories, but news carried by couriers was exclusive and easy to steal. With the Industrial Age news was transmitted via the telegraph and it was much more difficult to steal *en route* because it sent through a wire but it was often stolen when it was published. With the Information Age news is so multifaceted and transmitted in so many ways from so many sources that it loses its timelessness and originality almost instantly. News has a much shorter life and it loses its value faster than ever before. Above all, news is again easy to steal because of its electronic availability.

It has also become increasingly difficult to make a clear distinction between events, information, sources, and news. Most events are organized and "newsed," often even before they take place. Information is available everywhere, and its form often resembles the form of news. News sources are incredibly varied and potentially almost anybody can become a news source thanks to new media and communications technology. News is offered free from streetcorners to Internet nodes. Sometimes one needs to say no to more news in the 24-hour news cycle that is overcrowded with events, news, sources, and information.

Notes

1　A letter from W. Turner to Mr Moloney on May 23, 1935. Sir Roderick Jones papers, Section 2, Box file 2. Reuters' archive.

2　Sir Roderick Jones papers, Section 2, Box file 3, Reuters Archive.

3　US District Court In Equity No. 4 14–59. The AP (complainant) against INS (defendant) January 30, 1917. Brief on behalf of complainant. Sir Roderick Jones papers, Section 2, Box file 2. Reuters' archive.

4　US District Court In Equity No. 4 14–59. The AP (complainant) against INS (defendant) January 30, 1917. Brief on behalf of complainant. Sir Roderick Jones papers, Section 2, Box file 2. Reuters' archive.

5　R. Jones (1927) Statement. Conference of Press Experts, Fourth Plenary Meeting, League of Nations. Geneva, August 25, 1927. Sir Roderick Jones papers, Section 2, Box file 3. Reuters' archive.

5

Localization

Places in News

Stories, whether everyday or literary, serve us as means of mass transportation. (de Certeau 1984, 112)

Media and communication researchers have paid much more attention to "what" in news than to other questions. As Ferguson (1990, 164) observes, "the Lasswellian dictum of the communication process (which imitates the news formula) is blind to the temporal and historical/contextual aspects. There is no 'when' in who says what in which channel to whom with what effect, just as there is no 'where.'"

Schudson (1995, 14) writes that

> a news story is supposed to answer the questions of "who," "what," "when," and "why." But *understanding news as culture* requires asking what categories of people count as "who," what kinds of things pass as "whats," *what geography and what sense of time* are inscribed as "where" and "when," and what counts as an explanation of why. (emphasis mine)

Not only have communication researchers ignored "where," but they have understood "where" in a rather conventional way. To quote Hallin (1986, 109) "'where' seems to communication researchers a simple fact, as straightforward as it is uninteresting." There are instances, however, in communication research when researchers have addressed the question of "where." Carey (1989, 18), in making his influential distinction between the transmission and the ritual views of communication, indirectly touches upon the question of place ("where") when he refers to sharing, participation, fellowship, and the possession of a common faith as distinguishing characteristics of ritual communication. According to Carey (1989, 21), the model is "not of information acquisition," but of "dramatic action in which the reader *joins* a *world* of contending forces as an *observer* of the play" (emphasis mine). One of the ways the reader joins such a world is by identifying with places.

The concept of place is thus essential for media and communication studies. The theoretical work of several globalization theorists (for example, Giddens 1990; Harvey 1989) suggests that it is more important than ever before. As Giddens (1990, 64) puts it, "globalization can be defined as the intensification of worldwide social relations which link distant *localities* in such a way that local happenings are shaped by events occurring many miles away and vice versa" (emphasis mine). However, it is easily forgotten that in the nineteenth century electronic news already contributed to globalization and thus increased readers' sense of place. Nineteenth-century electronic news started to build the bridge between here and there by bringing the places where events occurred close to the readers of news.

Media and communication research often lacks a historical dimension. Most research concentrates on the twentieth century and thus fails to acknowledge that it was the first electronic media of the nineteenth century, news agencies, that changed concepts of time and place and became early agents of globalization. The electronic media in the nineteenth century were the first to decouple time and distance by bringing news from remote places instantaneously (Rantanen 1997, 615).

Unfortunately, when "where" has actually been studied in news, it has been restricted to traditional geography. The news flow studies written since the 1950s (for example, *The Flow of News* 1953; Sreberny-Mohammadi et al. 1985) started to consider the geography of news. They conceived the question of "where" in terms of states and followed the geopolitical borders of (nation-)states as drawn on maps. News flow studies were mainly interested in how different states were represented in news compared to their size or population, and even this interest was defined in terms of percentages. The news flow studies tended to ignore the significance of places and the role of news in constructing them. Only the debate about the diminishing power of nation-states in globalization has brought the importance of place to the research agenda.

An Alternative Approach: Geography Inside People's Heads

There are categories of place with equal or even more significance than states, such as regions, cities, villages, streets, roads, and home (Relph 1976,

21). As modern geographers have pointed out, geography can be constructed phenomenologically as a study of the relationship between people and the world they live in (Relph 1976, 5), that is of the *geography inside people's heads* (Crang 1998, 11). Phenomenological geography stands in contrast to traditional geography which, according to Soja (1989, 36–37), was primarily concerned with accumulation, classification, and the theoretically innocent representation of factual material describing the areal differentiation of the earth's surface. As Entrikin (1991, 13) writes

> The difference between the geographer's construction and that of the individual actor in everyday life rests primarily on the degree of self-consciousness of its creator and the choice of criteria. Therefore, the geographer's concern for an accurate description of the world may not coincide with the goals of an individual agent concerned with acting in the world.

The fundamental difference between traditional and phenomenological geography is that the latter is about people's own experience, how they feel about places, while the former is an outsider's view that claims to be objective because it is based on maps. News flow studies, which have classified the contents of news into categories and counted news on the basis of its geographic origin have thus echoed the practices of traditional geography. News was seen to be biased if there was more or less news from a certain country in proportion to its geographical size. News geography in the flow studies was always about nationality and about geographical regions, not about places. But, applying Relph's idea of geography inside the head, the study of "where" in news could not only be about geography in its traditional sense, but also about the *relationship* between people and places. Such an approach is potentially close to Carey's idea of ritual communication of "dramatic action in which the reader joins a world." If we are to think about how news connects people, place is an essential element, because it is, as Heidegger says, "the locale of being in the world" (Harvey 1993, 9).

No Sense of Place?

Meyrowitz (1985, 6) argued in his influential book, *No Sense of Place*, that electronic media affect us not primarily through their content, but by changing the "situational geography" of social life. He (1985, 115) writes

Changes in places in the past have always affected the relationship *among* places. They have affected the information that people *bring* to places and the information that people have *in* given places. Electronic media go one step further, They lead to a nearly total dissociation of physical place and "social" place. When we communicate through telephone, radio, television, or computer, where we are physically no longer determined *where* and *who* we are socially. (Emphasis mine)

Hence, Meyrowitz (1985, 308) concludes that the feeling of "no sense of place" has increased because "our world is becoming senseless to many because, for the first time in modern history, we are relatively without place, i.e. we are a part of a global world." Meyrowitz's thinking resembles that of Giddens (1990) and Harvey (1993), both of whom add another dimension to the shrinking of the world identified by Meyrowitz and others (originally by McLuhan). Harvey and Giddens name time–space compression or distanciation as an essential element of globalization. Harvey (1989, 239–259) talks about *time–space compression*, the objectification and universalization of concepts of space and time, and the annihilation of space by time. For Giddens (1990, 17–21) the concept is one of *time–space distanciation*, the distanciation or separation of time from space. In his view, in conditions of modernity, the level of time–space distanciation is much greater than in even the most developed of agrarian civilizations. Waters (1995, 58) has criticized Giddens's concept, because distanciation leaves the impression that time and space are becoming stretched, whereas it is rather social relationships which are becoming stretched across great distances. Waters further argues that new communications technologies are ensuring that transglobal social relationships are becoming more intense and robust, rather than stretched and attenuated as Giddens suggests, whereas Harvey's notion of the compression of social relationships (so that spatial distance becomes unimportant) fits the model of globalization much more closely.

Meyrowitz wrote his book well ahead of the globalization discussion. He ignored time, but refers to basically the same phenomenon. He, however, goes a step further than Giddens and Harvey by proposing that the consequence of time–space compression is "no sense of place." However, electronic news in the nineteenth century first *increased* readers' sense of place, by bringing them simultaneously news from many places. Rather than losing their sense of place, readers became more aware of place; they acquired a *new* sense of place. They consumed the news at home, but it came from distant locations.

Foreign news takes place elsewhere, and only makes sense if its readers understand the difference between here and there. We take "foreign news" and "domestic news" as given categories. The *Oxford English Dictionary* defines "foreign" in several ways. One definition is "a distance from home," another "something opposed to domestic," yet another something "alien in character, unfamiliar, strange." This is all oppositional to "domestic," which is defined as "intimate, familiar, at home."

Foreign news is also defined in relation to several of its aspects: (1) as home news abroad; (2) as foreign news at home; and (3) as foreign news abroad (Sreberny et al. 1985, 63). It could also be that the source of the news story is foreign and the actors in the story foreign. Usually the terms "foreign" and "domestic" news have been equalized with "foreign" as opposed to "national" news. This approach is based on taking nation-states as self-evident starting points for analysis, and on accepting uncritically that news stories are either "foreign" or "domestic," depending on whether or not they are taking place outside the borders of the nation-state where a medium is located. I have argued elsewhere (Rantanen 1992, 4) that this approach is false, since "foreign" and "domestic" are deeply interwoven, as are "global" and "local." These categories are important because they have an effect on what it is in news that is perceived as new.

The distinction between foreign and domestic is false in the sense that is presupposes that only foreign news comes from a distance, from a culturally "unknown" place – just because it is foreign. If we look, however, at the distances inside one nation-state, these are often greater than those between two locations in different nation-states. Measured in miles, London is further from Edinburgh than it is from Paris. News from Edinburgh is, however, "domestic," because it comes from within the United Kingdom, while news from Paris is "foreign." Thus when we talk about distance and overcoming distance, we are speaking not only of technological, but of cultural distance. As Anderson (1991) famously remarked, newspapers and news thus *regularly* and repeatedly remind citizens that they belong to the same nation-state.

But belonging has no meaning unless news offers readers a point of identification. These points of identifications have made and continue to make it possible for readers to be both "here" and "there" at the same time and thus strengthen their sense of place. Beck (2000, 72) uses the term place polygamy to describe a situation where people have access to several places rather than just one. He is referring to people who actually travel, but we can extend his concept to the news audience. The difference, of course, is that the news audience stays at home, while it is the news that travels.

Here we come to the question of mass-mediated social relationships (Thompson 1995, 81–118; Tomlinson 1994, 156–158). If we accept that all relationships are mediated (for example, by language) we are still left with the question of the difference between mass-mediated and non-mass-mediated relationships. Tomlinson (1994, 158) argues that a President whom we see on TV could never be familiar to us in precisely the same way as our next-door neighbor, or even as the distant person to whom we speak on the telephone. One reason, he writes, is that the President never appears to us as a dialogue partner. But even two partners in dialogue on the phone are very aware of the difference between their two locations. In non-dialogical relationships, such as news, the gap between the location of the news and that of its readers becomes even bigger. Readers, while they are reading the news, are closely tied to their own place. There was no illusion of being there as well as here among readers of the nineteenth-century electronic news printed in newspapers. The difference between here and there was clearly indicated by the place and date attached to each news story. There was no dialogue between the news and its readers; the relationship was based on an implicit contract that readers knew of the difference between their own location and the location of the news.

But the fact that news takes place somewhere else invites readers to engage with another place. When describing how Simone de Beauvoir read books as a young girl as a means of *translating herself into other worlds*, Rowbotham (2000, 8) uses Okely's term *dépayser* (to change scenery or disorientate) to describe the effect of books on de Beauvoir. As Rowbotham observes, the precision of French provides words for mental processes which remain ambiguous in the Anglo-Saxon consciousness. The idea in my analysis of changing places in news is best described by "changing scenery" (rather than by "disorientating" which connotes an uncertainty about place), although even that misses the capacity afforded by news consumption of becoming more conscious of these new places, whilst not actually changing places physically.

Home as Place

Place is fundamental to how we make sense of the world (Sack 1992, 5). People live in places, they miss places in which they have lived or stayed.

They need their own place in which they feel comfortable. As Crang (1998, 102) observed, people do not simply locate themselves, they *define* themselves through a sense of place. The concept of home comes very close to place. Home is a starting point for everything else. "There's no place like home" indicates the familiarity and emotional involvement we attach to our homes as places of our own. Crang (1998, 103) writes of places "Places provide an anchor of shared experiences between people and continuity over time." Spaces become places as they become "time-thickened." They have a past and a future that binds people together round them. The lived connection binds people and places together. It enables people to define themselves and to share experiences with others and form themselves into communities.

Even if people know their home/place best, visits to new places make them feel also closer to their home. People often talk of how they long to go back to the places they have visited. They carry mental pictures of these places and/or bring back photographs and souvenirs to remind them. Even if they have not been to a place themselves, knowing somebody from there (a relative, friend or pen pal) helps them to form an attachment to it. Still, despite possible attachment to other places, their own location and places far away are two different categories, although both kinds of place can be present in their minds. People need to feel safe at home, but at the same time may be curious about unknown places. Crang (1998, 47) writes that every travel story reflects the creation of a home, lost or returned to. In its familiarity, home can become restrictive and boring. People long for new places in order to liberate themselves. By identifying their homes they are also able to locate themselves in space, making sense of it by differentiating the known from the unknown.

Hence, people do make a distinction between here and there, although both are present in the human way of being. For Heidegger, *Dasein* ("being-there"), human existence, living one's life as a human being, always involves a place (Dreyfus 1995, 14). We live *here*, but increasingly we are able to reach *there* by means of transportation and communication. Heidegger uses the term *Entfernung* ("de-severence"), by which he refers to the abolishing of distance between things near and far (Dreyfus 1995, 130). As Scannell (1996, 167) writes, "de-severance attempts to capture the sense of what Heidegger calls *Entfernung*, which means something like to abolish distance or farness, i.e. to bring close, to bring within range." Scannell describes a possibility of radio as transforming spatiality; as bringing things close and hence within the reach of concern; as making the world (the great world beyond one's reach) accessible and available for oneself or for anyone. Although Heidegger wrote little about the media in *Time and Being*, making only brief remarks about radio and newspapers (for example, Heidegger 1995, 140, 164), the problem of *place* occupies a central focus in his thinking. The abolition of distance raises the fundamental question of how much our *Dasein* is shaped by the Other, who is not present but located far away. A place that is not ours indicates Otherness, because it is not familiar. For the vast majority of people in the world overcoming distance is mainly possible through mass-mediated social relationships. Here we come to the role of news in constructing place.

The External Characteristics of Place in News

Shaaber (1929, 1) writes that travelers were eagerly pumped for the news they brought from the places they had visited; that, indeed, it was often a matter at least of good manners, if not a duty, for a traveler to relate the news he had picked up, as fair return for hospitality. A standard way of finding the way by road across medieval Europe was to use an itinerary set out on along a roll on which *places* to be passed through were arranged in order, with an indication of the distances between them (Spufford 2002, 54). A letter or postcard from a place always indicates the difference between here and there, because it often starts with a reference to place and time (for example: "Helsinki June 6, 1859," or postcards with printed names of places, but almost never of countries). Newsbooks, letters, and newspapers followed this tradition, but there is not much information about the significance of place in standard media histories. It is as if place did not exist in news, although every news story started with a place and date. For example, a newsbook entitled *The copie of a double letter sent by an Englishe gentilman from beyond the seas, . . . containing the true auises . . . of the death of one Richard Atkins, executed by fire in Rome, the seconde of August, 1581* or, from 1601, *Newes from Ostend, of, The Oppugnation, and fierce siege, made by the Archeduke Albertus his Forces . . ., and Further Newes of Ostend*, or news published in *corontos* under rubrics indicating the place and date of origin: "From Venice, the 13. of Januarie" (Shaaber 1929, 183, 304, 312). The names of many newspapers, for example, the twice-weekly *London Gazette*, started in 1665, included their place of publication (Harris 1978, 83).

However, before headlines were invented it was place and date that separated the telegraph news (later added with time as 1.30 p.m.) from each other as shown in Figure 5.1. Electronic news became a travel story of the modern age in which time and place occupied an increasing role. Lukerman (cited by Relph, 1976, 3), in his analysis of the concept of place, writes about

REUTER'S TELEGRAMS.

——•——

The following Telegrams were received at Mr. REUTER's Office May 7th, 1859:–

BERLIN, Saturday, May 7th, 8 A.M.

Berlin is plunged in sorrow by the melancholy news that the Nestor of German science, the immortal Alexander von Humboldt, died yesterday at 8 p.m.

TRIESTE, Saturday morning, May 7th.

The Austrian Lloyd's steamer just arrived brings the following advices:

CONSTANTINOPLE, April 30th.

The Porte has culled in 50,000 Redifs. Omster Pasha has already quitted Bagdad *en route* for Constantinople.

ATHENS, April 30th.

The Grand Duke Constantine of Russia arrived here on the 26th ult.

Printed at Mr. REUTER's Office
1, Royal Exchange Buildings, City

Figure 5.1 Reuter's telegram, May 7, 1859. Published courtesy of the Reuters Archive.

the idea of location, especially as it relates to other things and places. Location, he claims, can be described in terms of internal characteristics (site) and external connectivity to other locations (situation); thus places have spatial extension, and an inside as well as an outside. The first part of my news analysis concentrates on the spatial extension of places, that is, how they are connected to other locations.

This flow of news from different places, published in random order and separated only by the date, time, and place, is worth closer examination. Obviously, not all news came by the telegraph; some still came by ship. The news from Constantinople and Athens took seven days to reach Reuter's office in London, while that from Berlin and Trieste arrived on the same day. More obviously than ever before, time and place became interconnected in news. The electronic flow of news created an impression of global space in which every place was simultaneously, and continuously, linked. This was the major achievement of electronic news transmission: it gave the impression of bringing the world to people instantaneously.

The places where the news came from had nothing in common except that they were all part of Reuter's network. However, despite the geographical distance between them, they were all interconnected to form a global news space. The news flowed like a stream, without interruption, from day to day, and later – when transmission became faster – from hour to hour. The names of the places where it originated varied, but the flow was endless and, to a certain extent, repetitious.

This repetition has been one of the main findings of news flow studies. Although these studies concentrate mainly on recent times, studies of earlier periods have shown that, for example, in the nineteenth century London, Paris, Vienna, and Berlin were the new leading centers for electronic news (Rantanen 1990). They emphasized that the concentration of news on these major capitals increased their significance as places. This is, of course, true, and was one of the early signs of the formation of the "global network society" (Castells 1996) which is mainly constituted of big cities. At the same time, the names of these places began to lose their significance, because the same names were repeated over and over again.

This rapid and continuous repetition of place-names brings us close to Meyrowitz's concept of *no sense of place* or Augé's (1995) concept of *non-place* or *placelessness* – what Relph (1976, 118) describes as "a meaningless flatscape." These terms, however, are usually used in connection only with supermodernity, i.e., with our contemporary time, not with the nineteenth-century modernity. Augé distinguishes between "place" (which is encrusted with historical moments and social life) and "non-place" (where individuals are connected in a uniform manner and where no organic life is possible) (Beynon and Dunkerley 2000, 35). For Bauman (2000, 97), non-places are places of consumption where consumers often share physical spaces of consumption such as concert or exhibition halls, tourist resorts, sports activity sites, shopping malls, and cafeterias without interacting. Bauman (2000, 102) writes

> "Non-places" share some of the characteristics with our first category of ostensibly public but emphatically non-civil sites, they discourage the thought of "settling in," making colonization or domestication of the space all but impossible.

Although Bauman (2000, 102) concludes that "never before in the history of the world have non-places occupied so much space," nineteenth-century news may provide a counter-example. What is common to non-places is that they are characterized by *mobility*. The difference between supermodern non-places and non-places in the nineteenth-century news lies in the ways in which they combine mobility and non-mobility. In the nineteenth century, for the first time, news traveled by itself, without a carrier, via the telegraph, while its readers did not move. In the twentieth and twenty-first centuries both readers and news are on the move; furthermore, readers can move, within their news consumption, to different locations, as happens on the Internet. Mattelart (2000, 108) writes

> Place is triply symbolic for it relates to identity, relationships, and history. It symbolises the relationship of each of its occupants with her/himself, with the other occupants, and with their common history. The multiplication of "non-places" is a characteristic of the contemporary world, places of traffic (highways, flight corridors), consumption (large supermarkets), and communication (telephone, fax, television, networks). The status of the consumer or lone passenger involves a contractual relationship with society. These empirical non-places that generate mental attitudes and types of relationship with the world belong to super-modernity, defined by contrast with modernity.

The readers of nineteenth-century news had a similar contractual relationship with the news to the consumers or lone passengers of the twenty-first century. They knew their place, they stayed at home, but the news invited them to "change the scenery." The first place-name in any news story proffered this invitation, based, of course, on the assumption that its reader recognized the place. However, these place-names mentioned at the beginning of electronic news items offer few possibilities of identification beyond the recognition of place. The headlines (or rather the datelines) of printed electronic news come closer to traditional geography, that is, to an outsider's view of places, a non-place. However, the places thus named form the global news space, a space made up of the world at hand, and the world in a form that makes sense, despite its objective randomness. The place-names at the beginning of electronic news items are there to be recognized, but it is the news story itself that constructs the location and identification of places.

The Internal Characteristics of Places in the News

To understand the significance of place in news it is important to go inside the news, its internal characteristics, to see how it is constructed. Events take place in a specific location, making location an essential part of how news constructs an event. According to Bell (1991, 198), time and place constitute the setting of a news event. Although he analyzes present-day broadcast news, his schema can also be applied to nineteenth-century news. It provides, furthermore, an opportunity to go beyond the major locales of the news, such as cities and towns, as analyzed in the previous section. The following example is a telegram by Mr Reuter on the occasion of the visit of the Russian Grand Duke Constantine to Paris in 1858.

To illustrate the constitution of time and place in this telegram, I follow Bell's schema.

The first place mentioned is Mr Reuter's office, without reference to its location in London, because that is taken for granted. In fact, Mr Reuter's office is what in news flow research is called the *source*, the agency that transmits the news. The first geographical place mentioned is Paris, together with the "when" (the date) that begins the news item. Place in news is obviously not the same for different people. As I pointed out earlier, news flow studies deal with the level of (nation-)states and make a distinction between different kinds of foreign news on the basis of location. The first place mentioned in a news story indicates its identification as domestic or foreign. In this particular case, if we use the categories of the news flow studies, the telegram will be classified as domestic news abroad (Russian Grand Duke visiting Paris) for Russian readers, as foreign news at home (Russian Grand

ELECTRIC NEWS.

———•———

The following Telegram was received at Mr. REUTER's Office Dec. 20th.

Paris, Monday evening, Dec. 20th.

The Grand Duke Constantine of Russia arrived to-day at ½ past 1 o'clock, visited the Emperor at 2 PM. and afterwards the members of the Imperial family.— His Imperial Highness then went to the Russian embassy, where he received the ministers, members of the nobility, &c. He will dine at the Tuileries this evening and afterwards visit the Opera *incognito.*

To-morrow a grand dinner will be given at the the Russian embassy, at which the Count Walewski, Marshal Vaillant, Minister Fould, Admiral Hamelin, and the Duke of Montebello will assist.

To-morrow evening at 8 o'clock the Grand Duke will return to Marseilles.

———————

Printed at Mr. REUTER's Office
1, Royal Exchange Buildings, City

Figure 5.2 Reuter's telegram, December 20, 1858. Published courtesy of the Reuters Archive.

Duke in their country) for French readers, and for other readers as foreign news involving both a foreign city and a foreign actor. As Hallin (1986, 110) and Bell (1991, 200) have remarked, place-names often express "who" rather than "where" – a political actor rather than a physical territory.

Table 5.1 The construction of place and time in news

Place	Time
Mr Reuter's Office	Dec. 20th
Paris	Monday evening, Dec. 20th
(Grand Duke Constantine of Russia)	today at $\frac{1}{2}$ past 1 o'clock
(Emperor)	at 2 PM
(Imperial Family)	afterwards
Russian embassy	then
Tuileries	this evening
Opéra	afterwards
Russian embassy	to-morrow
Marseilles	to-morrow evening at 8 o'clock

Likewise, actors often express place. In this case the Grand Duke Constantine of Russia, or the members of the Imperial family, indicate the status of both actor and place. The Grand Duke represents simultaneously Imperial Russia in France.

The place-name is the most general level of place. The news also constructs lesser places which allow the reader to locate the event in relation to her- or himself. Obviously,at the more general level, places have different significance for different readers. Those who live in, or have visited, Paris, know where the Opéra or the Tuileries are, while others may or may or not be familiar with these from reading or hearing about them. Readers who live in, or have visited, Paris, probably know the location of the Russian Embassy, although they may not have seen it as synonymous with the Russian state, as it is in this case, and as is the Grand Duke Constantine. Marseilles belongs to the same category of place as Paris, and is familiar to many readers as a French city, but again very few readers who do not live there, who have not visited it, or who have no connection to it, know more about it. Only through the construction of places, such as the Opéra, the Tuileries, or the Russian Embassy in this story, does news makes sense of places. These are elements of non-place that have actually become the landmarks which distinguish any capital. All capitals have places that everybody recognizes.

What is worth noticing is that all the places in the telegram (except the cities of Paris and Marseilles themselves), are *public places* created and known through common experiences and involvement in common symbols and meaning (Relph 1976, 34). The Opéra, the Russian Embassy, and the Tuileries are all symbols of power and influence. How much they are shared symbols is another question, but they are known as Parisian landmarks even to those who have never visited. News, by mentioning the names of public places, offers an opportunity for identification.

It is also important to note how time and place become one in news. Place and time are closely interwoven, going hand in hand throughout the news. The first time given here is the date of arrival of the telegram at Mr Reuter's office. Since this is the same as the date in the following line (Paris, Monday evening, Dec. 20th), it shows that the telegram originated on that same day. This was, of course, very important in the period when news agencies were trying to convince their clients that they could deliver their news as fast as possible. The whole story is structured around the concept of the present. As Bell (1991, 201) writes, some references in news stories situate events in absolute or calendar time (in this case December 20th), while others situate it in relation to other events ("then," "afterwards"), and still others are deistic, with the present as their reference point ("this evening," "tomorrow"). The dates, times, temporal adverbials all create the feeling that if it is not happening right now, it happened very recently. The story is written in the past tense, but the expressions of time give the impression that the readers are following the Grand Duke step by step. This also intensifies the here-and-now atmosphere of the telegram.

Places and Non-Places

In this chapter, I have argued that electronic news creates both placelessness and a new sense of place. When we look at the places in the datelines at the beginning of electronic news stories, seeing how they flow one after another, it is easy to agree with Relph's and Augé's ideas of placelessness or non-place. Relph (1976, 58, 98) claims that mass-identities of place are the most superficial identities of place, offering no scope for empathetic insideness and eroding any existential insideness by destroying the basis of identity with place. He talks about an inauthentic attitude toward place being transmitted by media, which directly or indirectly encourages placelessness. Relph defines the media effect as a weakening of the identity of places to the point where, although they do not look alike, they feel alike, and offer the same bland potential for experience.

News flows offer almost no point of identification except recognition by readers who know the name of the place. All places evoked in news stories look and feel alike, but together form the global news space available to readers in different locations. The great benefit of electronic news – too often ignored – is that it brings the world to its readers, thus acting as one of the earliest vehicles of globalization. De Certeau (1984, 112) writes of the railroad as allowing us to move through place and of train windows as allowing us to see from a great distance. Electronic news, like other stories, serves as a means of transportation, but its readers are not moving (unless they are traveling) – they remain in their place. The place-names cited in news stories allow their readers to see, but – as de Certeau observes of travel – not to touch, because the more you see, the less you hold. In contrast with travel, news has only points of departure and destination. The in-between place, as Schivelbusch (1978, 34) calls it, disappears in news transmission, because it is the news that travels, not the readers. The annihilation of time and space in electronic news makes possible the simulation of events as if they were happening here-and-now. It is the reader who stands between news and home, in the in-between place, and makes the difference between the two.

When we look at the places inside news, we see how news offers points of identification by guiding its readers through places by naming them. The place-names in the news are mostly names of public places, which serve as a means of de-severence for readers, abolishing the distance between the place, which is there, and readers, who are here. The places cited are often universal places, to be found in almost every major city, and are also symbols of power, such as government buildings and embassies. The level of generalization is similar to that found in guidebooks for travelers. The difference between news and guidebooks is, again, mobility, or the lack of it, since travelers really go to new places, while news stories only imitate travel, with their readers remaining in place.

In electronic news we find the contradiction of being "here-and-there" at the same time. Its readers are here, but news comes from there. News tries to build a bridge between the two places by creating a "here-and-now" atmosphere. Despite these efforts, readers' daily lives are elsewhere, at home, and they are aware of it. This "divided being" (Soja 1989, 135), which news stories, in their imitation of travel, have increased, exemplifies the existential essence of modern and, increasingly, postmodern humans, and it is a phenomenon that began as early as the first electronic news in the nineteenth century.

6

Nationalization

News and the Nation-states

True and unbiased news – the highest moral concept ever developed in America and given the world. (Kent Cooper, AP's General Manager (Cooper 1942: x))

Billig writes that in the established nations there is a continual "flagging," or reminding, of nationhood (Billig 1995, 8–9). One of the ways to remind citizens about their citizenship is to flag news. National news stories serve as flags constantly reminding citizens of the national agenda. Many authors before me, most notably Benedict Anderson (1991), have noted the role of media in constructing the nation. As Anderson writes, the simultaneous act of reading newspapers allows people who do not know each other to imagine themselves as belonging to the same nation. Anderson's powerful argument is based on the behavior of those who consume the news, not that of its producers. In communication and media studies, the argument has been almost entirely different: national news and especially the organizations that produce it are seen as not only worth establishing, but also worth protecting, without problematizing their role as producers of the imaginary. Many UNESCO documents, from both the 1950s and the 1980s (see for example UNESCO 1953; Sreberny-Mohammadi et al. 1985) recognize the importance and role of national news agencies and/or national newspapers in producing news that protects the interests of the nation-states where they are located. Curiously national news is seen at the same time as something that is inherently more "objective" than international news or news coming from neighboring nation-states.

Hence, the concept of objectivity has been often associated with the nationality of news. The nationalization of news is thus a relatively modern invention that started with the industrialization of news. Jean Chalaby

(1996, 303) has argued that the modern conception of news as related to the "objective description of facts" is an Anglo-American invention of the nineteenth century. Before that time, news was primarily cosmopolitan and by its nature concentrated mainly in big cities. What we now see as "natural" was invented only 200 years ago, but simultaneously in many countries with different political systems. In this chapter, I present three case studies on the development of "German," "Russian" and "US" news agencies of the nineteenth and early twentieth centuries, each of these being very different from the others politically and culturally, but using the same argument for the nationalization of news. It was the competition between them and the interference of their respective national governments that forced agencies to turn into national agencies and news into national and international news.

Early History in Europe

The first European news agencies were founded in the mid-nineteenth century in Paris, Berlin, and London by Messrs Havas, Reuter, and Wolff, who saw their agencies primarily as private companies and their product, electronic news, as private goods created in order to make a profit. From the very beginning of their activities they transmitted news from and to other *cities*. What is remarkable in their early arrangements was that these were originally cosmopolitan, rather than national or international.

This doing business across borders with the new weightless good, electronic news, was without precedent. Messrs Havas, Reuter, and Wolff may have had the illusion that they were making their business arrangements simple, but in practice these proved complicated. If they were initially under the illusion that they were doing business beyond the national, between the cities where they were located and other cities, not only their governments, but they themselves and competing agencies all over the world were soon to object to this. As a result, the three agencies established a system of agreements (1869–1934) that gradually divided the world's news market in accordance with their spheres of interests. Hence, the international system of news exchange became so powerful that even governments saw the need to become involved, either directly or indirectly, in the news business.

There has not so far been a single country where the government has not been involved in some phase in news transmission, usually in times of internal or external crisis. Such interference took place in two main ways: through technology or through agencies. In both cases, the interference could be direct or indirect, but was always carried out in the *name* of national interest and against another country's national interest. Hence, the cosmopolitanization of news soon came to be opposed by the nationalization of news. The nationalization, in contrast to the cosmopolitanization, of news is defined by a situation where governments, in the name of national interest, support institutions such as telegraph companies and agencies so that these may serve primarily the interests of a particular nation-state. This can happen either indirectly, through ownership, licenses, discounted fees, subsidy, or political support, or directly, through establishment of or taking over a telegraph company or an agency.

The State and News

Since the birth of news agencies over 170 years ago there has been much debate about the ideal form of ownership. Traditionally, the state's role has been seen almost solely in terms of forms of agency ownership. In the past, news agencies were often divided into three main categories on the basis of their ownership: (1) private; (2) co-operative; (3) government (state). The first European news agencies were mostly private, often named after their founders (e.g. Fabra in Madrid, Havas in Paris, Reuter in London, Stefani in Rome, Tuwora in Vienna, Wolff in Berlin). Later, almost every agency was named for its nationality (e.g. Russian Telegraph Agency, Swedish News Agency, Norwegian News Agency), indicating that the nationality of news was the primary factor.

Government agencies are almost as old as other ownership forms. The first private agency was Havas (1935), the first co-operative agency the Associated Press (1846) in New York, and the first state agency the KK Telegraphen Korrespondenz-Bureau in Vienna which started in 1860 to distribute articles to the newspapers published by the Austro-Hungarian government (Dörfler and Pensold 2001, 15). Although the state's role varied from country to country, government-run agencies were soon widely acknowledged, for example, in Germany, Russia, Italy, and the Balkans. Many news agencies that were commonly regarded as private, nonetheless had close connections with their respective governments. Reuters is a case in point: the London-based agency enjoyed significant government subventions throughout much of the twentieth century (Read 1999).

Although the first news agencies in Europe were private, governments and the state in different countries soon became involved in their operation. First, governments needed news, political and economic, domestic and foreign, for more informed decision-making. Second, they needed a transmission belt for the dissemination of their own news and views (Rantanen 1990, 30). Third, and perhaps most importantly, governments had a profound interest in helping to project a positive image of themselves both at home and abroad (Boyd-Barrett 1986, 68). Hence there were several reasons why news needed to be nationalized and could be nationalized through organizational intervention.

It would be wrong, however, to view the relationship between governments and news agencies as uni-directional. In fact, it was bi-directional. There were several reasons why news agencies needed governments. First, news agencies naturally wanted governments as clients to bring much needed subscription fees. Unlike most private newspapers, the state was a reliable and long-term client. Second, news agencies wanted news about and from governments and they wanted to have it earlier than anybody else. This is why they wanted to have exclusive rights to official government news (Boyd-Barrett 1980; Rantanen 1990). Third, they needed the support of government authority against competitors in home or foreign markets. Government intervention, whether financial or ideological, direct or indirect, was often a decisive factor in competition with domestic and foreign news organizations.

As Rantanen and Boyd-Barrett (2001, 39) write, previous research on news agencies has often understated the complexity of ownership forms among news agencies. The division into private, co-operative, or government agencies is simply not enough. First, a private agency may be quoted on stock markets, so in a limited sense it is then "public" (which is what happened to Reuters when it became a public company in 1984). It can also benefit, as most did, from direct or indirect subsidies. Second, there are also different kinds of "co-operative" structures: an agency's ownership may be limited to a range of different media, yet still be a private company.

The Associated Press was formally constituted as a not-for-profit co-operative news agency for newspapers, but still was able to exclude them from its membership if they competed with existing members. Some co-operative agencies comprised only newspapers, others included government, private and even labor representatives. Third, private agencies can function on a not-for-profit basis, while government agencies may seek profits. The degree of government involvement in state agencies varies greatly, as do political arrangements that articulate and often constrain a state's involvement in day-to-day agency operations (Rantanen and Boyd-Barrett 2001, 39).

State interference is often through technology. Thus, we can only understand the nationalization of news if we explore the ownership and control of transmission technology and agencies together, not separately as has been done in the past. Traditionally, the ownership of a news agency has been seen as the most important single factor influencing its independence. However, since technology and news are so closely connected, the state may also exert its influence through technology. The telegraph companies were mostly state-owned. With the British Telegraph Act of 1868, which authorized the Post Office to purchase and operate all telegraph companies in the UK, the US and Canada became the only nations where the telegraph remained private (Du Boff 1984, 59). Telegraph companies were "nationalized" almost from the beginning, so whatever the ownership form of agencies, they always had a relationship with the state through technology.

The simple fact that the telegraph lines connected places in different countries and thus formed a connection between them soon led to their regulation in the name of the state. Telegraph lines were considered national property, but international co-operation demanded collaboration with other states. The first international telegraph conference was organized in St Petersburg in 1875. Cables that ended in another country and crossed the territories of other countries were difficult to control. If countries were at war, cables were confiscated, as happened when World War I broke out and the British cut the German cables in the English Channel and took over their cables elsewhere (Headrick 1991, 141). From the state's perspective, the telegraph was "easy" technology to control compared to the wireless, which did not need lines or cables, but only airwaves that could not be forced to follow national boundaries but "spilled over." Like the telegraph, radio waves soon became state property, even if briefly, in the US.

In this chapter, I analyze three case studies in order to give empirical support for my argument about the nationalization of news. These are agencies with three different ownership forms, but each facing a stage where either the state interferes, using the nationality of news as a reason, or the agencies themselves use the nationality of news to ask the government to interfere.

The First Interference: Wolff Goes State

One of the most famous early examples of state intervention concerned Reuter's attempt in 1865 to penetrate Wolff's market by establishing branch offices and even, in 1869, trying to purchase the whole agency. It was not untypical in the early years that Havas, Reuter, and Wolff all actually founded branch offices in several countries. The competition between other local agencies, on the one hand, and between Havas, Reuter, and Wolff, on the other, was one of the main reasons for the transformation of Wolff into a state-owned agency.

Reuter and Wolff had signed their first contract, covering only financial news, in 1856, and extended this in 1859 to political news and to include Havas. Under the terms of the 1859 agreement, Havas had a monopoly for news transmission to the cities of Augsburg, Würzburg, and Stuttgart. Reuter meanwhile was rapidly expanding its network. Together with Havas, Reuter had also founded an agency in Brussels with branch offices in Antwerp and Ghent, and Reuter bought Delamar's agency in Amsterdam. Reuter also established branch offices in Hamburg, Frankfurt, and Hanover (Basse 1991, 36–37). Wolff bitterly resented Reuter's expansion into its market and established a secret agreement with the Prussian government that all political messages should be counted as official, and thus given priority on all state lines over press telegrams from Reuter or from other press correspondents (Williams 1953, 23).

Reuter, who had once himself lived and worked in Berlin and Aachen and knew the market probably better than anybody else, went even further: he founded Telegraphischen Bureau Norddeutchland under the leadership of Hofrat Alberts in Berlin and Süddeutschen-Korrespondenz-Bureau in Munich, with several branch offices. In 1865, the Royal Hanoverian government signed a concession to land a cable on the island of Norderney, in the East Frisians, off the north coast of Hanover, and Reuter was given the right to establish an office in Hanover (Storey 1951, 42). The Norderney cable was opened for traffic in 1866, and an agreement made for new land lines which Reuter would build to Hanover and to Hamburg, Bremen, and Cassel, for the agency's exclusive use (Williams 1953, 21). Within a year the Hanover office was bringing Reuter, from telegram fees paid by outside customers alone, a revenue of £2,000 a month (Storey 1951, 43). As Basse (1991, 38) observes, Reuter was particularly successful in the cosmopolitan-oriented Hansa cities, where it won a steady clientele, Hamburg being the most important of these for Reuter. Reuter gave up Hamburg only under the 1898 agreement, but Wolff had to pay Reuter in return 12,000 marks annually (Ingmar 1973, 33).

In response to Reuter's expansion, on June 10, 1869 Wolff's business manager, Richard Wenzell, turned to the Prussian government for help. The Prussian government and "patriotically" oriented (Ingmar 1973, 17) bankers, von Oppenheim, von Magnus, and von Bleichröder, together with Wolff, concluded a new institutional arrangement to protect the home market against foreign interference. A new company, Continental-Telegraphen-Compagnie (CTC), whose main stockholders included the government, banks, and Wolff, Wenzel, and Theodor Wimmel, was founded. Nine years later, the founder of the agency, Bernhard Wolff, had severed all links with the company (Höhne 1977, 48). A subsequent new treaty between the agency and the government also guaranteed the new agency certain privileges, most important of which was priority for its telegrams in the telegraph traffic. This advantage, added to an exclusive right to official news, enabled CTC to defeat its domestic rivals and become more competitive on international markets. For its part, CTC promised to give the authorities free copies of all its dispatches. The agency also agreed to submit its telegrams to prior censorship (Naujoks 1963, 610; Rantanen 1990, 30; Basse 1991, 39–41).

Following an offensive–defensive agreement between CTC and Reuter in 1887 (Palmer 1976, 343), the Italian prime minister, Francesco Crispi, in 1888 approached Bismarck to form an alliance against Havas, between CTC, the Austro-Hungarian Korrespondenz Bureau and the Italian Stefani – all by that time state-controlled agencies – in order to increase their operational freedom, especially in the Balkans. Stefani was in the Havas territory and fully dependent on it. For Bismarck and Crispi, the financial dependence of German and Italian official agencies on the French agency was humiliating (Palmer 1976, 345). Unexpectedly, the end result was an alliance between Reuter, CTC, and Korrepondenz Bureau, but excluding Stefani, against Havas. According to Bismarck, despite the "Havas-Reutersche Lügenfabrik" (Havas-Reuter Factory of Lies) (Ingmar 1973, 59) and the fact that "Reuter did not lie less than Havas," Reuter was after all "ein alter Hannoveran" (an old Hanoverian) (Ingmar 1973, 53–54) and thus a better partner than Havas.

However, none of these actions succeeded in breaking the dominant position of Reuter and Havas in relation to CTC in their mutual agreements. They also show the power of news agencies: even governments were unable to bring significant changes in the framework the most powerful agencies had created. But what they did establish was a tradition where government interference in news transmission was viewed as justified in the name of national interest and this resulted in the foundation of further state-owned agencies around the world.

CTC ceased to operate when the National Socialist Party rose to power. The German government already had 51 percent of CTC's shares and the remaining private shares were transferred to the German government. CTC was amalgamated with another agency in 1933 and a new agency, Deutsche Nachrichtenbüro, founded. Although this was nominally a shareholder company, it came fully under government control. (Reitz 1991, 213–216).

The Second Interference: Agencies in St Petersburg Go State

Another example is St Petersburg, where several private and co-operative agencies had existed since 1866, but the government finally took over in 1904. The main reason for this was the agencies' dependence on CTC in Berlin (Rantanen 1990, 130). Since that time Russia has had an uninterrupted tradition of government agencies, lasting until today.

In Imperial Russia, as in many countries, news agencies started as private firms, but were later taken over by the government. There were internal and external reasons for governments' actions and they often used one to justify the other. Russia is in many ways an extreme case of state ownership, since the state has controlled both technology and agencies for most of their existence, but even there we can see periods of different combinations of state and private firms. However, it is fair to say that, from Imperial times to the present, Russia has had an exceptionally strong state involvement in both technology and news.

In 1857 Wolff started to deliver political telegrams to three St Petersburg newspapers, which shared the costs for Wolff's service. Then Reuter started to deliver its news to St Petersburg. As a result, Wolff and Reuter were competing against each other. Wolff even petitioned to establish its own agency in St Petersburg, but the Russian government decided to favor a local entrepreneur, granting permission to Russkoe telegrafnoe agentstvo (Russian Telegraph Agency), founded in 1866 by Konstantin Trubnikov, who wrote in his petition:

> At present, all political and commercial telegrams are received solely from *Prussia*. We shall not even discuss the fact, that, under such circumstances, Russia is in total dependence on a *foreign* telegraph agency. One also encounters the following problems here. First, the Prussian agency transmits to Russia news dispatches as it sees fit, and, consequently, in this case, it can act contrary to *Russian interests* and solely in the interest of Prussia itself. [...] Second, news dispatches from the various states to Prussia are interpreted solely in terms of the latter's needs. As a result, Russia is put on the same level as other states. However, in telegraph news dispatches, Russia's own interests should absolutely have the first priority. (Rantanen 1990, 85, my emphasis)

Trubnikov received foreign telegrams from Reuter, and Wolff's telegrams disappeared from Russian papers. However, as early as the following year some papers became dissatisfied with the agency's service, established their own agency, and decided to become Wolff's clients once more. After the government shifted its permission to the new agency, which received an exclusive right to the electronic transmission of foreign news to St Petersburg and Moscow, Wolff became the main source of electronic news from abroad. This situation was confirmed in the 1870 agreement between Havas, Reuter, and CTC, which defined St Petersburg and Moscow as CTC's territory. Every new agency to be founded in St Petersburg was obliged to make an agreement with CTC.

Eventually, the situation where CTC was the sole provider of telegraph news from abroad justified the government's desire for tighter control over news transmission. By giving an exclusive right to operate to only one agency at a time for a certain period, and by subsidizing its operations, the government was in a position to take over if it wished. A memorandum from the Ministry of Finance in 1902 observed

> The RTA is not an equal member of the cartel of the international news agencies, but a branch office of the Berlin Wolff agency, through which the Russian agency both receives and transmits all its news. Telegrams from St Petersburg may be shortened or completely changed by the Wolff agency: hence news from Russia to foreign countries passes though a *German* prism. News from abroad comes to our country in the similar way. [...] Such a situation is intolerable, because our foreign trade cannot be completely autonomous so long as telegraph news about commerce is in the hands of *foreigners*. (Rantanen 1990, 127, my emphasis)

The existence of state-owned agencies has been justified by very similar arguments, used in Russia and elsewhere since the nineteenth century. In an article entitle "The Slaves of Reuters" written by one of the executives of ITAR (Informatsionnoe telegrafnoe agentstvo Rossii) – ITAR-TASS from 1995 – the author bitterly complains about Reuters' increasing influence in the market and the inability of ITAR-TASS to compete:

> Not by accident, in many countries measures have been taken to forbid, in general, Reuters' independent operations in their territories. [. . .] Our information space is absolutely open: all these [foreign] agencies can operate here as they like. This is the whole story. In this way *alien, information empires* are create *in our territory.* (Rantanen 2002, 79–80, my emphasis)

The Third Interference: US Government Supports Associated Press and United Press through Technology

The US situation was very different from that in other countries, since the state did not own the telegraph as it did in European countries. The same applied to news agencies in the USA, which were always either co-operative or privately owned, but never state-owned. New York City's Associated Press (NYAP) origins could be traced to joint harbor activity by some newspapers in the 1820s and 1830s. Later most of these papers engaged periodically in associations to operate horse expresses. The first use of the telegraph was in 1846, which is generally considered the founding year of NYAP (Schwarzlose 1989, 90). Later US agencies always claimed that they were fiercely independent from the government. As Kent Cooper, Associated Press General Manager, testified in 1927:

> So far as the Associated Press is concerned, of course it has no government connection and never has had, and it has never has asked and does not ask any preferential treatment from any government.[1]

However, even in the US there were several instances when the state intervened, although in more subtle and indirect ways than, for example, in Germany and Russia. After all, the US agencies managed to do what German and Russian agencies did not: to become leading world agencies after World

Table 6.1   The countries controlling world cable facilities in 1919

Country	Percentage	Miles
UK	51.0	140,000
US	26.5	72,000
France	9.0	25,000
Germany	7.5	20,000
Denmark	3	8,400
Spain	1	3,000
Japan	1	2,000
Italy	1	2,000

Source: US Senate, *Subcommittee of the Committee on Naval Affairs* 1919, 28.

War I. The change in their status was preceded by a campaign for US-owned transmission technology and US-owned news.

At the beginning of the twentieth century, the UK was still the leading power in electronic communications technology. By 1907, more than 38,000 nautical miles of submarine cables had been laid, mostly under British ownership and control. This gave rise to interference by the US government because "the *British* government found itself in a position to censor and control the interchange of intelligence between the most civilized people. Thus, in more than fifty years, the *British* government had acquired control of international communication" (*The Radio Industry* 1928, 71). The countries controlling world cable facilities were, in order, as shown in Table 6.1.

Table 6.1 shows the situation after World War I. In the mid-nineteenth century the situation was still quite different. Thus, when cable news first became available in the United States, British companies dominated both news content and technology. From the US government point of view, the situation was extremely expensive, fraught with delays, and of course out of national control.[2] This was a particular concern in South America where the US government had growing political and financial interests. As was testified before a House of Representatives Committee in 1917

As late as 1878, all messages from the United States to South America had to be sent via Europe, passing through a *British* cable. [. . .] The *British* trade supremacy has been controlled by means of communications. There is no question that *London* is the cable center of the world. Being the cable center of the world, it is the news center of the world, and part of the *British* position throughout the world is due to the fact that *London* is the great center for distribution of news. (Rogers 1919b, 110, my emphasis)

The Introduction of New Technology

The new technology of the time, wireless telegraphy, again brought changes. It was an efficient way of distributing news over wide areas and at a lower cost than the telegraph. Unlike the telegraph, radio – or wireless – communication enabled users to send messages for simultaneous reception at a number of destinations. Messages could be either received by the telegraph authorities or delivered to the addressees or be picked up by the addressees through their own receiving apparatuses (UNESCO 1956, 19).

The wireless had first been used successfully for news reporting by the *Daily Express* of Dublin, Ireland, to report the Kingstown Regatta in July 1898. The Atlantic was first spanned by a wireless connection in December 1901, between Poldhu, Cornwall, and Cape Breton at Glace Bay, Nova Scotia (Desmond 1937, 102). By 1908, a transatlantic radio service between Ireland and Nova Scotia was in operation. Before the US entered World War I, its navy's high-power transcontinental, transpacific chain was in operation. This network consisted of stations at Arlington, Virginia; San Diego, California; Darien, Canal Zone; Pearl Harbor, Hawaii; Guam in the Mariana Islands; and the Gavite in the Philippines (*The Radio Industry* 1928, 75). But this was not enough; it was important to have a more comprehensive network under US control. As Walter S. Rogers testified:

> America needs more cables, and it needs radio facilities. It would be a crime, from which the newspapers would be one of the principal sufferers, were trans-Atlantic and trans-Pacific radio to pass into the *control* of some *foreign* owned corporation and of some *foreign government*. Such foreign control would determine the services and rates for the *American* press and might result in preferential service or rates to agencies in competition with *American* agencies and newspapers. (My emphasis)[3]

On the Pacific side, however, there was thus only one cable, connecting the US with the Far East. The rates for news transmission by cable were prohibitive, ranging from 33 cents per word for a service subject to all sorts of delay to over $3 per word at the urgent rate for expedited service and guaranteed quick delivery. Under such conditions, there could be no regular news service across the Pacific; the Far East, including the Philippines, received international news (including news from the US) through London and Japan, and news came out of the Far East by the same circuitous route.[4]

For the first time in the history of electronic communications in the United States, the state took an interest from the start in the new technology. As was said,

> England had historically been mistress of the seas and still controlled international transportation. Thanks to her cables, she had long dominated the field of communications. The wireless telegraph was beginning to threaten the long reign of the cables, but if Britain could also control this younger prodigy, she would own at the outset two of the three essentials for world dominance. (Young 1929, 21)

It was also important that the US companies did not rely on only one form of communication because "no nation of any importance does not have more than one system today of international communication" (Winterbottom 1929, 302).

By proclamation, on the day following the US declaration in April 1917 of war against Germany and entry into World War I, President Wilson directed the Navy to take over all wireless stations in the US and its possessions that were not already under the control of the Army (Archer 1938, 123). Furthermore, the government became involved even in content production. The Division of Wireless and Cable Service, know as Compub, started to transmit US news abroad in September 1917 (Creel 1920, 251–260).

Government control far outlasted World War I. Until 1924, the Naval Communication Service handled practically all news transmission in the Pacific, the commercial rate being prohibitive to any satisfactory service. For example, AP sent a daily average of about 1,000 words from San Francisco to Honolulu and about 800 words to Manila. The radio activities of the Naval Communication Service were taken over by the Radio Corporation of America in July 1925 (*Fourth Pacific Science Congress* 1929, 12). The introduction of wireless telegraphy reduced the rates to an average of 25 percent lower than competing cable rates (Sarnoff 1928, 104).

Following the example of Havas, Reuter, and Wolff, the world's radio market was also to be divided. The Radio Corporation of America, RCA,

Table 6.2 The difference between former and present rates per word for international communication from the US

To	Former rate per word ($)	Present rate per word ($)	Saving per word ($)
England	0.25	0.20	0.5
France	0.25	0.23	0.2
Germany	0.35	0.25	0.10
Italy	0.31	0.25	0.6
Norway	0.35	0.24	0.11
Sweden	0.38	0.25	0.13
Japan	1.22	0.72	0.50
Hawaii	0.35	0.25	0.10
Brazil	0.50	0.42	0.8
Argentine	0.50	0.42	0.8
Venezuela	1.00	0.60	0.40
Colombia	0.65	0.40	0.25
Liberia	0.98	0.50	0.48

Source: Sarnoff 1928, 104.

with General Electric as the major stockholders, bought out the British holdings in American Marconi (the company had been controlled by the British) and agreed to divide the world: the British Empire for Marconi, Latin America for the US, Canada to be shared between them, and the rest of the world open to both (Headrick 1991, 182), thus assuring RCA a virtual monopoly on US international radio communication. The government control of all wireless land stations was a trump card that forced the British to sell. International communication would become the chief function of RCA (Czitrom 1982, 70). By 1921, the Radio Corporation of America had succeeded in establishing no fewer than five transatlantic wireless circuits from the US to the UK, Norway, Germany, France, and through Hawaii to Japan (Sarnoff 1928, 102). As a result, the US had daily communication with 25 countries. Wireless messages were now sent from New York to the UK, France, Germany, Italy, Norway, Sweden, Holland, Belgium, Poland, Turkey, Liberia, Puerto Rico, St Martin, Venezuela, Colombia, Dutch Guiana, Brazil, and the Argentine. From San Francisco, wireless messages were being sent to Hawaii, Japan, the Philippines, the Dutch East Indies, French Indochina, and via the Philippines to Hong Kong and Shanghai, China (Sarnoff 1928, 102).

The Navy service was still much slower, however, than that furnished by either RCA (all-wireless) or the Commercial Cable Company (all-cable), both of which were operating between the US and the Far East. A United Press dispatch by RCA was now received in Tokyo a few minutes less than 12 hours after it was filed. Its one virtue was the fact that it saved 6 cents per word in comparison to the next cheapest rate obtainable. The word-rate from New York to Tokyo by Navy radio (and over the land wires and submarine cables which it supplemented) was 24 cents, while by RCA the rate was 30 cents. The rate by cable was 38 cents.[5]

Congress evidently intended that the radio should act as a common carrier in the handling of these news reports, since their chief value lay in their being free from government censorship. However, the Navy Department had not got away from war policy and felt that it was responsible for the transmission of anything in these reports that might damage a friendly nation. Because of this policy, and in line with general orders, a few news items were held up by naval officers of the sending nations.[6]

Congress induced the Navy to grant authority for the use of its wireless facilities for the transmission of commercial and news messages between points which could not be served by privately owned stations. It stipulated that general commercial business must not be conceded at lower rates than those granted by private stations, and that a low rate might be granted for news transmission. Under that authority the Navy announced a rate for news messages of six cents per word from San Francisco to Manila, and three cents from San Francisco to Honolulu.[7]

Justifications for the Nationalization of News

World War I also marked a watershed for both AP and United Press, and both continued to expand abroad. The justification for entering the Far East market was again mainly made in three different ways: (1) that it was not seen through US but British eyes, (2) that the cable connection via London was too slow; and (3) that the agencies found the cable rates to Asia prohibitively expensive. As a contemporary later testified

> Years ago the news in the Far East, both incoming and outgoing, was practically controlled by Reuter, which is the Great *British* news agency, and some five years or more years ago there was an arrangement that was made between

Japan and Reuter under which Reuter would retire entirely from Japan, and Japan took absolute control of the incoming and outgoing news of Japan [...] At the time the Great War opened the only information which the Far East secured of this country was through Reuter and Kokusai. The Reuter report was prepared by an *Englishman in New York*, they were blue pencilled and reedited by an *Englishman in London*, was sent through a circuitous cable route down to Africa, recabled to Shanghai, then again blue pencilled and re-edited by an *Englishman*, and *in Shanghai* they had the most bitter feeling against *Americans* at the opening of the war and years afterwards. (McClatchy 1919, 6, 8, my emphasis)

As was testified, trade follows communication and transportation (Winterbottom 1930, 287), and the establishment of better, faster, and cheaper communication with the Far East was seen as important not only by the agencies but again by the government. AP and UP faced a similar situation in the Far East to that which they had faced in South America before the war. AP had an agreement with a Japanese agency, Kokusai, which was a government agency and restricted to operating under Reuters. The Far Eastern news market belonged to Reuters, and AP was not allowed to operate there – unlike UP, which was free to move (Rantanen 1994, 19). Again, the government urged the US agencies to work together to promote national interests. As Walter Rogers wrote:

I made a suggestion to the great press associations of the world that they take an interest in communications with the idea of extending the news service, and I was particularly interested in getting news service from the United States to the Orient on some permanent basis, so there might be some chance of the two sides of the ocean understanding each other. I believe Mr Stone, of the Associated Press, and Mr Howard, of the United Press, are exchanging notes with other various connections throughout the world with the idea of center for distribution of news. (Rogers 1919b, 110)

The Inconvenient Combination of the Cosmopolitan and the National

The nationalization of news did not, and does not, necessarily mean only the etatization of news, i.e., direct state involvement; it was also used as an ideological justification for state interference. In numerous instances, news

agency directors have used nationalism to justify the foundation or existence of their agencies. Even Havas, Reuters, and Wolff, which started as
non-national organizations, soon began serving as national organizations.
However, of the three, Reuters never served as an officially recognized
national agency, because another organization, the Press Association
(founded in 1868) served that function in the UK.

The uneasy relationship between the international and the national is
one of the contradictions most news organizations carry within themselves.
They have claimed to be, at the same time, national institutions with a
mission to their home country and international organizations without a
bias toward any country. Sir Roderick Jones wrote of Reuters.[8]

> The Agency is recognized in the most remote places of the earth as a typical
> *British* institution conducted upon honest and responsible lines, and as such,
> in the ordinary pursuit of its business, it has done probably more than any
> other single institution abroad to create *British* atmosphere and to spread
> *British* ideas. For nearly half a century all over the East and the Far East
> Reuter's has been either the only service of news distributed or, as in recent
> years, the dominant and paramount service. As such it is conspicuous every-
> where, from the Mediterranean to the further coasts of Japan, as a daily and
> hourly expression of *British* enterprise and *British* influence, not only through
> the press but on the Exchanges and in the markets. (My emphasis)

However, it was also necessary to make claims about Reuters' non-
Britishness in order to sell news to non-British clients. Jones contradicts
himself in another statement and needs to use the word cosmopolitan
instead of international:

> While *British* in origin, the Reuter service is *cosmopolitan* in its complete
> freedom from bias and partiality. It is detached, judicial, objective, and
> absolutely neutral, and this, coupled with its unchallenged reputation for
> accuracy and independence, makes it acceptable to *foreigners* of every race.[9]
> (My emphasis)

The growing conflict between the US Associated Press (AP) and Reuters in
the early part of the twentieth century was significantly concentrated
around the issue of the nationality of news. AP criticized the power of
Reuters on the grounds that they represented the world as seen through
British eyes. Kent Cooper, AP's general manager, who rose to resist Reuters'
dominance, was critical of Reuters precisely because it was a British

company. He used Reuters' Britishness as a justification for his actions against it. AP, for its part, claimed that Americanism resulted in a superior news service. Cooper wrote:

> To The Associated Press I give credit for the creation of what turned out to be the finest moral concept ever developed in *America* and given to the world. That concept is that news must be truthful and unbiased. (Cooper 1942, 18–19, my emphasis)

Cooper, like Jones, took the view that only news originating from the country where an agency was located could be truthful or unbiased, and that as a consequence the nationality of news becomes the primary factor in defining its objectivity. They were not alone in their argumentation. It has been used many times over the years since the foundation of the first news agencies. An argument close to this is that a country is misrepresented in news because a news agency located in another country is disseminating news about it. This second version has been repeated on a number of occasions, most recently in the UNESCO debate in the 1980s around the New World Information and Communication Order, when developing countries criticized Western agencies for misrepresentation on the basis of the nationality of news (Cuthbert 1980). However, it was Cooper, whose agency ironically later became a target of similar criticism from developing countries, who wrote

> So Reuters decided what news was to be sent from *America*. It told the world about the Indians on the warpath in the West, lynchings in the South and bizarre crimes in the North. The charge for decades was that nothing creditable to *America* was ever sent. American businessmen criticized The Associated Press for permitting Reuters to belittle *America* abroad. (Cooper 1942, 12, my emphasis)

The other argument that was used several times against other agencies was their connection with governments. This argument is very close to the first and second arguments about the nationality of news. On the one hand, government and the nationality of news go closely together and cannot be separated, because in principle both should represent the nation. On the other hand, the nationality of news is seen as distinctly different from the national government. This independence from government should guarantee the impartiality of news in the same way as news is more impartial if it comes from the country where a news organization is located.

News agencies were seen as less independent if they were government-supported or -owned. The most obvious cases were news agencies in the former communist countries, for example the Soviet TASS that was officially "to announce" news from the government. Curiously – and here is another contradiction – TASS was founded, like many other government-owned agencies, on the basis that foreign agencies misrepresented news because they were not located in the particular country concerned. Whilst the telegraph freed the agencies from the constraints of geography, it could not liberate news from the constraints of the nation-state. This simply became impossible because of the importance of news for nation-states. As a consequence, despite the fact that the first news agencies started their operations on a non-national basis, news soon became a national issue everywhere.

The Many Functions of National News Agencies

As Boyd-Barrett (2000, 301) has noted, national agencies serve significant functions. First, they provide affordable domestic and international news services to national and local media; their news portfolios typically aim to be comprehensive with respect to the representation and interests of the major different constituencies of the nation-state. Second, they are important and privileged sources of news for national political, economic, and financial institutions. Third, they serve as a conduit for the services of international news agencies to local, domestic media and also feed back local and national news to the international news agencies, and thus can influence the international representation of their individual nation-states.

The role of national news agencies has been adequately analyzed, but not sufficiently critically assessed, except in countries with totalitarian regimes. The traditional division of news agencies into international and national has taken for granted that news agencies need to serve national functions. However, only the most recent globalization debate has questioned the national as a self-evident starting point. There is no reason to presuppose that news agencies or any other media organizations should necessarily serve the interests of nation-states. However, the history of news agencies shows how the first electronic media were transformed in most countries into the vehicles of nation-states. This happened because the independence of news agencies was vulnerable: they were dependent on the technology required to receive and send news.

As a result, in most countries there have been periods when news agencies have been under either the direct or the indirect influence of the governments in their countries of location. Even in the most unlikely countries, such as the US, where the media's independence from government has always been celebrated, such periods can be found. The two US agencies, the co-operative AP and the private UP, were both influenced, despite their different forms of ownership. The government was able to interfere through technology, but also by persuading the news agency directors that they all shared similar interests. It was in the name of a greater common cause that news agencies not only accepted, but even embraced, government interference, which was often carried out in very subtle ways, giving the impression of a joint project rather than of government influence.

Studying the historical development of news agencies shows us the power of the national. US President Wilson was convinced, after attending the peace conference in 1917 in Paris, that future world pre-eminence would be determined by three major factors: raw petroleum, transportation, and communications (Young 1929, 21). And so it was. The battle over the nationality of electronic news that had already started in the mid-nineteenth century was to go on for another 100 years. The latest technology, the Internet, may bring a change. If it does, it will not happen without another battle.

Notes

1   *Editor & Publisher*, August 13, 1927, 7.
2   A message from New York via London to South America required from six to fifteen hours, while directly from New York it required only two or three hours. The rate between New York and Valparaiso, via the European route, was $6.00 per word. World War I brought down the full rate of the direct service to $0.50. *A Half-Century of Cable Service to the Three Americas* 1928, 22 and 39.
3   *Editor & Publisher*, July 17, 1919, 9.
4   *Editor & Publisher*, December 24, 1921, 6.
5   *Editor & Publisher*, July 1, 1922, 6.
6   *Editor & Publisher*, March 12, 1921, 6.
7   Ibid.
8   Sir Roderick Jones papers. A note on Reuters. For private information only. Printed by Waterlow and Sons Limited, London, Dunstable, and Watford. Reuters archive, box file 97.
9   Sir Roderick Jones Papers. Broadcast address in Johannesburg by Sir Roderick Jones on February 26, 1935. Reuters archive, box file 13.

7

Epilogue

Today Was Yesterday

The young say they avoid serious factual. Notably they are watching less news. Young audiences to news bulletins on all channels have declined significantly over the last five years.

TV and newspapers play a constant role in an over-55's life. They watch and read news practically every day. Over 55s are the heartland of news. They make up the vast majority of local news viewers and believe it is important to read a newspaper every day. (BBC Commissioning 2006[1])

This book was written in many locations around the world. Among the places I spent time writing was, in 2006, San Felices de los Gallegos in Spain, a remote village of 600 people near the border with Portugal. I had my laptop with me, but no access to the Internet. The only visible public clock was on the church tower in the village square. The church bells rang on every hour to remind people of the time. Since it was the time of a festival, the Festival of El Noveno in commemoration of the population's freeing from taxation by the Duke and Duchess of Alba[2] on May 11, 1852, the bells rang even more frequently. What better place to think about the changing temporalization of news from the Middle Ages to the Information Age?

Another place where I spent time writing, also in 2006, was Los Angeles in the US, where daily, on Bus No. 14, I would see, above the bus driver's head, a digital clock with date and time, and the time changing as the minutes went by. I would also see many of my fellow passengers nonetheless looking at their watches, thinking about their own individual time and the personal events that marked it out.

On the bus we would hear an automated message telling us about the next stop and whether it had been requested by a passenger. Some of my fellow passengers would be listening to music through headphones, while others were reading their newspapers. Some of us would look at the TV screen, showing Transit TV's Moving Entertainment and a live map of the bus route with red spots illuminating the next stops. Transit TV also showed advertisements, cooking clips, crossword puzzles, and news in Spanish and English. The news was from Reuters and at the beginning of every news story it showed the place where the event was located. There was no sound, but there I read the story, with date and time, about the earthquake in the Philippines.

How was my experience different from the experience of a traveler somewhere else, or in previous times such as the Middle Ages? She would not be traveling by bus, but would still be traveling in a crowd, either on foot or by coach (carriage). Unlike me, she would probably talk to her fellow travelers, exchanging information with them about the place and their possible previous experiences there. Perhaps she would entertain her fellow passengers by inventing amusing stories. They would have to be "new stories," of course, because the people traveling with her preferred new stories to old.

Occasionally these travelers would meet new people, at inns or when changing horses, and new stories would be exchanged. They could listen to news singers at street corners in towns. However, they would not necessarily know how old these stories were, since time was not then measured at such short intervals as it is today. A story's newness was judged by whether it had been heard before.

But there would be no moving pictures, no stories updating themselves like those on the screen on our contemporary bus journey. Stories did not then arrive among the passengers unannounced or uninvited. Above all, they did not introduce another timeframe, different from that of the passengers' present journey. Travelers then were blissfully unaware of different time zones and events taking place at that very moment far away from where they were. When they learned about such events, it was often through stories of things that had already happened a long time ago. The influence of events on people's immediate lives was remote, since there was no shared time, common to far-away events and their own lives.

With the latest media and communications technology such as the Internet, news and its transmission have again profoundly changed. Although researchers disagree about the consequences of this transformation for journalism, they generally agree that a fundamental change is taking place. Many of us now live in the digital age, although all the earlier forms of news are still alive: oral, script, printed, and electronic. Technological convergence has multiplied the ways in which news is gathered and transmitted and combined all earlier forms with the latest. With the advance of new technologies, there is now more news than ever before. The ability to communicate cheaply on a many-to-many, one-to-one, one-to-many and many-to-one basis creates problems for those who are trying to make their living by selling news, and for those who try to consume the ever-increasing amount of news. The biggest impact on broadcast and satellite news delivery in recent years has been that of the emergence of new technologies, in particular the Internet and digital television.

Comparing two periods, distant from one another, the Middle Ages and the Information Age, we can highlight the differences and similarities between the two, ask what has changed and what has not. This chapter sets itself the task of doing this, and of outlining the options emerging from current developments. It argues that we need to re-conceptualize news because news as we knew it no longer exists. The present situation challenges in four different respects the ways in which we think about news. First, traditional news is losing its audience. Second, new technology is being used to collect, transmit, and comment on news. Third, the concept of time in news is changing, And finally, all this is changing the role that news is playing in contemporary societies.

Old News Is Losing Its Audience

There is already research that shows young people in many Western European countries shifting from traditional media to the Internet. The Internet reaches young people in the 15–24 age group far more effectively than traditional media, especially newspapers. 63 percent of adults in the UK had accessed the Internet in the three months prior to February 2006. This is much higher amongst 16–24 year olds with 83 percent going online.[3] In the UK, 91 percent of respondents said that they still find television a useful source of news, compared with 71 percent for newspapers, 59 percent for radio, 13 percent for the Internet and 13 percent for magazines (Hargreaves and Thomas 2002, 5).

Research also shows that people are increasingly "grazing" very many news sources, rather than regularly relying on the same source. People feel least informed about their own localities. Only a minority, 43 percent, think television news represents all sections of society fairly (Hargreaves and Thomas 2002, 5). We are witnessing the end of the mass audience for traditional news, especially among young people (Hargreaves and Thomas 2002, 11–12).

Several researchers have noted that there has been a structural decline in public interest in traditional news. In the United States audiences for network peak-time news bulletins have fallen from 90 percent of the television audience in the 1960s to 60 percent in 1993 and 30 percent by 2000. More recently, Internet news, once largely the province of young, white males, now attracts a growing number of minorities. The percentage of African Americans who regularly go online for news has grown by about half over the past four years (16 percent to 25 percent). More generally, the Internet population has broadened to include more older Americans. Nearly two-thirds of Americans in their 50s and early 60s (64 percent) say they go online, up from 45 percent in 2000. Newspaper readership among young people continues to be relatively limited. Among those under age 30, just 23 percent report having read a newspaper yesterday. This is down slightly from 26 percent in 2002 and stands in marked contrast to the 60 percent of older Americans who say they read a newspaper yesterday. Young people are more apt to read a magazine or a book for pleasure on a daily basis than they are to pick up a newspaper.[4]

Other forms of news, such as 24-hour television news, news on the Internet and even news by word of mouth, now play a larger role. In the UK, TV is still far and away the main source of news for most people: Two thirds of them say it is their main source. The proportion of people saying the Internet is their main news source has trebled – but only to 6 percent. And radio has declined by a third as people's main source of news. Asian and Black groups are less likely than the population at large to watch TV network and in particular to listen to radio news. Both are more likely to watch 24-hour news channels, while Asians are much more likely to consume news on TV channels from the sub-continent and news from the Internet (Philips 2007). The Internet is most popular among young people (18 percent) and women (12 percent). It is also very popular among Asians, 37 percent of whom make use of it. Word of mouth is a more frequent source for women and younger people; 43 percent of 16- to 34-year-olds name oral communication as a useful source of news. According to researchers, the Internet appears to be emerging as the news "home" for those who feel under-served by conventional mass media (Hargreaves and Thomas, 2002, 46–47).

One quarter of Internet news consumers in the US use foreign sites published in a country other than their own country of residence (Best et al. 2005, 52). In the US nearly one third of visitors to the typical newspaper website come from outside the traditional geographical offline distribution area: this percentage increases for major national news sources such as the BBC, which reports that more than 50 percent of its online traffic originates from outside the UK (Best et al. 2005, 53). The Internet news audience – roughly a quarter of all Americans – tends to be younger and better educated than the public as a whole. People who rely on the Internet as their main news source express relatively unfavorable opinions of mainstream news sources and are among the most critical of press performance. As many as 38 percent of those who rely mostly on the Internet for news say they have an unfavorable opinion of cable news networks such as CNN, Fox News Channel, and MSNBC, compared with 25 percent of the public overall, and just 17 percent of television news viewers.[5]

All this research indicates that there have been many drastic recent changes not only in the consumption but also in the *production* of news.

New News?

As early as in the 1980s US dailies started to experiment with personal computers, television, facsimile, and even regular telephone calls as alternative means of providing information to the general public (Boczkowski 2004, 4). Since the inception of the World Wide Web (WWW) in the early 1990s, it has increasingly been used as a news medium. The second wave of online journalism started in 1991, when the WWW standard was released by CERN and even more importantly when the WWW began to be widely accessible through the availability of a free, Windows-based browser – Mosaic – in 1993 (Brake, 2008). However, the WWW is not a news producer, but a new form of technology used for the transmission and reception of news. The provision of news content is a separate role. I discuss here three different ways in which the WWW is a vehicle for news: (1) the provision of online news as an additional service by traditional news media; (2) search engines; and (3) weblogs.

Old New News Media

Traditional media, such as newspapers or news agencies, were quick to start using the new technology. For example, by 2001 readers could access approximately 3,000 online newspapers from the US and more than 15,000 from outside the US (Best et al. 2005, 53). According to the World Association of Newspapers, web audiences for newspapers have grown by 350 percent in recent years (Feuilherade 2004). The latest UK figures, from 2008, show how rapidly the situation has changed. The *Mail Online*'s unique user numbers increased 165 percent year on year to 17,903,172. In the same period, the readership of *Telegraph.co.uk* increased by 65 percent to 12,348,706; that of *Sun Online* grew to 13,322,535, up 40 percent from January 2007, and that of *Times Online* increased by 39 percent to 15,087,130. *Guardian.co.uk* remained the highest traffic website with 19,708,711 readers, a rise of 26 percent year on year (Kiss 2008).

The news received through these websites was not necessarily new. For example, when the *New York Times* was launched on the Web in 1996 it mostly featured articles from the printed paper (Boczkowski 2004, 74). An overwhelming share of the content found on these sites merely reproduces that found in the offline products of the same news media. Only 3 percent of online news sources charge a subscription fee for the viewing of their content (Chyi and Sylvie 2001, 245). Van der Wurff's study of four European countries concluded that online newspapers are still searching for their role. They perform several functions at the same time. Their front pages "market" the print newspaper, provide short news items and guide the reader to other content on the same website, and sometimes on other websites. The news items presented on the front page cover more or less the same geographic areas as those on the front page of the printed newspaper, though with less variation. Online newspapers differ more from printed newspapers in the functionalities that they offer than in terms of content. (van der Wurff 2005, 188).

What then is new about the old media's use of the WWW? Boczkowski (2004, 185–186) concludes that there seem to be at least three potential effects of the online environment on the content and form of news. First, instead of being primarily journalist-centered, online news appears increasingly to be user-centered. Second, instead of being fundamentally a monologue, communicated unidirectionally, online news appears increasingly to include unidirectional statements within a broader spectrum of ongoing conversations. Third, in addition to the local and national emphasis online news also appears to have a local presence. Fourth, I would add, the definition of what was strictly defined as international, national, and local news or news sources is rapidly changing.

Search Engines

Van Couvering (2008a, 177) divides the history of search engines into three different periods. First, a period of *technical entrepreneurship* from 1994 to late 1997; second, a period which was characterized by *the development of portals and vertical integration* from late 1997 to the end of 2001, in which major media companies and network providers attempted to buy their way into the search arena; and finally a period of *consolidation and "virtual" integration* from 2002 to the present day. Originally, search engines were called "navigation aids" to help Internet users who were feeling lost and also show them the history of their search (where they had been on the Net) (Lie and Liebenau 2000, 52). Services such as AOL, Yahoo! News and Google News are also major search engines that search specifically for news. The Google News site requires no human editors – unlike AOL or Yahoo! News. The Google search engine ranks results on the basis of the number of inbound hyperlinks that a site receives (Carlson 2007, 1019). It searches and browses 4,500 news sources that are updated continuously. The service is available internationally in 40 languages or regionalised versions.[6]

Search engines only select news from existing news sites; they do not themselves gather or produce news. Matheson calls them an apotheosis of the telegraph and news agency news conventions (Matheson 2004, 460). However, news agencies did themselves produce news. Carlson (2007, 1025) writes that news search engines grant users the ability to actively seek information in a two-way flow. He writes

> No news product exists outside of the news consumer, only a database of stories. The news consumer selects among these through searching by topics, which introduces a new level of audience activity as they choose both a topic and then stories on that topic from the search engine-generated list. This process invites a rethinking of the role of the audience in journalism. The presentational authority concept implies that journalists dictate an interpretive order to the news. In contrast, Google News's emphasis on access and diversity is predicated on viewing news audiences as actively creating their news environment. It is this disconnect between a news audience selecting from a preformed news product versus seeking news through supplied search terms that provides the basis for the tension between traditional media and news search engines.

Table 7.1 Unique visitors to top US online news sites (monthly average), 2006 vs. 2007

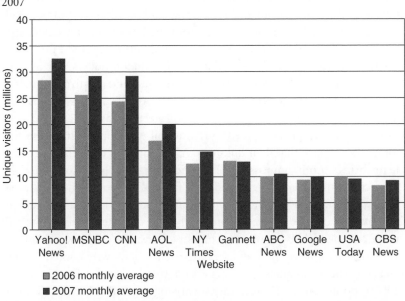

Source: The State of the News Media 2008. www.stateofthenewsmedia.org/2008/narrative_online_ownership.php?cat=4&media=5, accessed October 27, 2008.

Hindman, Tsioutsiouliklis, and Johnson (2003) argue that that a handful of heavily linked sites may dominate political information on the Web. Paterson (2006) argues that Google News could not exist without mostly reproducing news agency content. According to his study in 2001, news portals/aggregators showed no substantial mediation of agency content, with their text duplicating news agency text for an average of 68 percent of the content studied. By 2006, the average amount of measurable verbatim news agency use by these services had risen to 85 percent. Paterson (2006) concludes that the apparent diversity of original reporting in international news on the Internet is increasing, but the actual diversity of original reporting is decreasing or remaining static. This longitudinal comparative analysis of international news stories from major news websites with original wire service stories reveals a continuing scarcity of original journalism and a near-total dependence by major online news providers on news agency reporting and writing.

Google's dependence on traditional news agencies has been indirectly demonstrated through several lawsuits against the company (Paterson

2006). In 2005, Agence France-Presse (AFP) announced a lawsuit in the United States and France against Google for continuously breaching their copyright. AFP claimed that Google News unlawfully incorporated AFP photographs, headlines, and excerpts from the beginning of articles. Also, AFP argued, Google News removed photo credits and copyright notices, in violation of federal law. The suit was for 17.5 million dollars. For its part, Google claimed AFP's headlines were not "original and creative" enough to be protected under copyright law. "Typical AFP headlines are factual, simple, and contain only one idea – unprotectable as a matter of law." Google, however, quickly agreed to remove all AFP content from the site. Google also argued that their linking to AFP content at the websites of AFP clients brings profit, not loss, to AFP, which increases the possibility of the American courts seeing aggregation as "fair use" of copyrighted material (Paterson 2006). Google and Agence France-Presse reached an agreement over the use of AFP's materials in April 2007. The new agreement "will enable the use of AFP's news wire content in new, innovative ways that will dramatically improve the way users experience news wire content on the Internet," the companies' statement said (Oates 2005). Van Couvering (2008b) points out that it is hardly surprising that AFP settled, in view of the growing importance to most news organizations of the online traffic that search engines point their way – Google could in theory act as a *de facto* news censor.

It is thus not surprising that the Associated Press opted to negotiate with Google, rather than to sue over the use of its copyrighted material. Google argued that, because Google News is an aggregator, the company is not obliged to reimburse news outlets for linking to their content. Finally, Google agreed to pay Associated Press for use of its news stories and pictures, but argued that the AP content would be the foundation for a new product that would merely complement Google News. Thus Google maintains that the deal supports its original stance on fair use (McCarthy 2006).

Table 7.2 supports Paterson's data and gives support to his claim that the two remaining world/global agencies that have maintained their status as leading news providers for online media are Reuters and AP. If this is true then, rather than five world/international/global agencies, we now have two online global agencies. However, the mutual dependency between news agencies and search engines is changing the perceptions of news audiences which appear to see news aggregating websites as the sources of news instead of as collections of it (Brake 2008). Interestingly, in the US ratings for the online sites of the major national news organizations are

Table 7.2 Top US newspaper-related sites from appearance at Google News, April 2008

1	The Associated Press
2	*New York Times*
3	Voice of America
4	Reuters
5	CNN
6	BBC News, UK

Source: www.newsknife.com/ accessed October 27, 2008.

substantially higher than ratings for the news organizations themselves. For example, among online users who could rate, fully 54 percent give CNN. com a high believability rating, while only 40 percent give the same rating to CNN. With ABC News, 44 percent of online users rate the network's website highly believable, compared with 29 percent who give the same rating to the organization itself.[7]

Weblogs

The weblog is a form of writing that is unique to the Web, reliant on what is arguably its key characteristic: the hyperlink. Matheson (2004, 448) writes that a weblog is characteristically rich in hypertext links to other sites, and that the term "web log" and the statements by early "bloggers" suggest that this kind of webpage developed as a record of the user's latest browsing, which was made available for others' interest. Its most visible organization of material on the page used to be mainly chronological, rather than hierarchical (Matheson 2004, 448). However, many blogs do now have, as well as the main chronological organization, links in their sidebars to hierarchical and topical organization of their content. This is a very sought-after function and one that the online form and hyperlinks are good at, of course – the same set of items can be accessed and explored in more than one way – and has been a big selling point for some blogging software (Morris 2008).

News is not the most important feature in blogging. A phone survey of US bloggers found that most of them focused on describing their personal experiences to a relatively small audience of readers and that only a small

proportion focus their coverage on politics, media, government, or technology. Most bloggers do not think of what they do as journalism. They
say they cover a lot of different topics, but when asked to choose one main
topic, 37 percent of bloggers cite "my life and experiences" as a primary
topic of their blog. Politics and government ran a very distant second with
11 percent of bloggers citing those issues of public life as the main subject
of their blog. Entertainment-related topics were the next most popular
blog-type, with 7 percent of bloggers, followed by sports (6 percent), general
news and current events (5 percent), business (5 percent), technology (4
percent), religion, spirituality or faith (2 percent), a specific hobby or a
health problem or illness (each comprising 1 percent of bloggers). Other
topics mentioned include opinions, volunteering, education, photography,
causes and passions, and organizations. Blogs, according to the survey, are
as individual as the people who keep them. Most bloggers are primarily
interested in creative, personal expression – documenting individual experiences, sharing practical knowledge, or just keeping in touch with friends
and family (Lenhart and Fox 2006).

McIntosh (2005, 387) writes that many bloggers take the view that professional journalists are being disingenuous in *not* making their personal
beliefs and opinions clear to readers and letting the readers make their own
decisions on the value of the content based on their disclosures. According
to a recent study, a majority of blog posts either assemble material from
elsewhere, with only general comments and some analysis of such material,
while only a handful of posts could be said to be on-the-scene observation.
Blogs, while dominated by citizen communicators, in fact rely heavily on
professional news sites and stories by journalists associated with professional media organizations. (Reese et al. 2007, 247, 257). A one-week study
also found the sources for stories on these sites tended to differ from the
mainstream press. Blogs by non-journalists proved to be the most popular
source, making up 40 percent of the stories. Nearly 31 percent of stories
originated on sites such as YouTube and Technorati that also offer citizen-
generated content. Mainstream media, by contrast, made up just 25 percent
of articles on these sites. Wire services, such as the Associated Press and
Reuters, accounted for 5 percent of them.[8]

However, the old media are also increasingly using the techniques of
blogging in order to change the nature of their own reporting (Cowling
2005). The first known use of the format for a breaking news story in the
US was the *Charlotte Observer*'s report of Hurricane Bonnie in 1998.
By mid-2004, the American Press Institute listed more than 400 blogs

Table 7.3 Percentage of US citizen-run sites with at least one link to various types of sites

	Blog sites	News sites	Total sites
Link with traditional news organizations (newspaper, TV, etc.)	40%	24%	34%
Link to citizen news sites	28%	48%	34%
Link to citizen blog sites	60%	56%	58%
Links to commercial news sites	20%	4%	14%
Link to commercial blog sites	27%	4%	19%
Number of sites	39	25	64

Source: The State of the News Media 2008. www.stateofthenewsmedia.org/2008/narrative_overview_audience.php?cat=3&media=1, accessed October 27, 2008.

published mainly by journalists. Among blogs associated with traditional media, in particular, the overwhelming majority of links led to other mainstream media sites (Singer 2005, 176, 187). In the US fully 95 percent of the top 100 newspapers included blogs from reporters in March 2007, up from 80 percent in 2006, according to research conducted by the Bivings Group. In 2006, the latest year for which data are available, traffic to blog pages on the top newspaper websites surged. According to data from Nielsen//Net Ratings, the number of unique visitors to blog pages on the ten most popular newspaper sites grew 210 percent from December 2005 to December 2006. Collectively, those visitors made up 13 percent of total traffic to these websites.[9]

As Matheson (2004, 455) observes, the news text stands almost in the stead of the event, gaining status by claiming to know "what happened," positioning newspapers as "the arbiters of events in society" (Zelizer 1993, 80). The weblog, by contrast, is a source of information, "unedited, unabashedly opinionated, sporadic and personal" (Palser 2002). Matheson argues that the distinction is important because it allows us to think whether this is true and whether a "less cooked" story allows us to participate more in constructing events than a "polished" news story (Matheson 2004, 455).

There are conflicting views about the influence of blogs on journalism. Singer argues that they are being normalized and have become an enhancement of traditional journalistic norms and practices (Singer 2005, 193). However, other authors have argued that Weblogs challenge traditional news reporting (Matheson 2004, 451; Cowling 2005) by

1   providing a space for journalistic thinking for which institutional jour-
    nalism provides little room;
2   offering new feedback mechanisms to mainstream news media;
3   reducing the reliance of the mainstream news media on official sources;
4   forming new interactive relationships between groups of readers that
    are not spatially limited and are less limited by time;
5   inverting traditional editorial processes;
6   providing a more democratic, interactive space.

Blogging is often seen as the empowerment of traditional news audiences through their ability to become news commentators. As Singer writes, the question of "who is a journalist" online will only become more, not less, provocative as roles, norms, and practices become increasingly fluid (Singer 2005, 193). This, in turn, challenges the profession and especially the education of journalists.

The Concept of Time in News is Changing

The concepts of hypertextuality, multimediality, and interactivity (Deuze 2003, 205) can be applied to all online news, no matter to which category it belongs. All types of online news thus contribute to the changing concepts of time. Because they are also linked to each other, the difference between event, news, and audience changes. Hypertextuality changes the structure of news. Networks exist not only between, but also within news services. As Bolter writes, on the subject of the differences between "traditional" writing and writing on a computer: "If linear and hierarchical structures dominate current writing, the computer now adds a third, the network as a visible and operative structure." Bolter acknowledges that, even in traditional writing, the network has been an organizing, though latent, factor, more like "reading between the lines" (Bolter 1991, 113). Traditional news sources had similar organizing structures – as shown in Chapter 5 – which were much more visible and recognizable as a news genre (where, when, who, what). However, on the Internet hypertextuality adds a third structure of multiple times and places.

Bolter argues that time is a resource for the computer, just as coal is a resource for the steam engine. He (1984, xi) considers the computer to be the defining technology of our age, just as clocks and steam engines were the defining technologies of Western Europe in the seventeenth and nine-teenth centuries (Lee and Liebenau 2000, 48). The difference between clocks and computers is that "an ordinary clock produces only a series of identical seconds, minutes, and hours; a computer transforms seconds or microseconds or nanoseconds into information" (Bolter 1984, 102–103). Time is no longer a single fixed reference point that exists externally to events. Time is now "information" and is choreographed directly into programs by the central processor (Bolter 1984, 102–103).

With computers, we enter the age of "multiple times" (Turkle 1984, 13). As Rifkin (1987, 13) writes

> Every programme has its own sequences, durations, rhythms, and its own unique time. While the clock established the notion of artificial time seg-ments – hours, minutes, and seconds – it remained tied to the circadian rhythm. The clock is an analogue of the solar day, an acknowledgement that we perceive time revolving in a circle, corresponding to the rotation of the earth. In contrast computer time is independent of nature: it creates its own context. A digital timepiece displays numbers in vacuum – time unbound to a circadian reference. Computer time then is a mathematical abstraction that attempts to separate us from the pulls and periodicities of the natural world.

According to Sandbothe (1998), our spatio-temporal ways of world-making are not a rigid, uniform, and ahistorical apparatus. Linear time is said to be typical in monochronic cultures, while non-linear (multi-layered) time is typical in polychronic cultures. In the former people do one thing at a time, while in the latter several things are done at once (Lee and Whitley 1999, 17). Mumford (1934, 14) argues that the clock, not the steam engine, was the key machine of the modern industrial age. In the industrial age there was a clear distinction between work and leisure: work on five or six days a week from nine to five, while the rest was personal time (Lee and Liebenau 2000, 48). Clocks were set to collective time, even when some of those clocks came to be watches worn on the person. Col-lective time was one of the outcomes of the industrial age, as compared to the agrarian age.

Like clocks, news is both public and private in its consumption. In the Middle Ages news singers sang for audiences on the streets, and early news-papers were read aloud for small groups of people in open spaces and in coffee houses. Gradually the reading of newspapers became more private, and they were often read at the breakfast table before their readers left for work. Radio news broadcasts were repeated hourly and functioned like clocks on church towers: they told their audience the time, along with the latest news. Later, the TV nine o'clock news became a marker of clock time almost everywhere where there was television, and families gathered together to watch it. Even if consumed privately at home, news had a mass audience that read, listened to, and watched the same news at the same time. The news was about events, but news itself became an event. Media organizations decided what time news was to be released, and although individuals could choose the moment they wanted to have news, it was not available all the time. News time became regular and predictable. News marked time in the same way that clocks did.

Several authors have noted how the Internet has created a new sense of time that is not linear. Sandbothe (1998) writes that in the net's countless meeting places there is no unitary, somehow natural, time which partners in communication can presuppose to be self-evident. Internet time has stopped existing as the kind of linear, monolithic structure it was during the era of railways and telegraphs, and exists instead in many different layers (Hongladarom 2002, 241). Hongladarom gives the example of computers coming equipped with a connection through the Internet to one of the several available NTP (Net Time Protocol) servers which tell the client machine the time according to the time zone set by the user. The clock in these computers is not set by referring to any locality, but through the network by connection to an NTP server very far away (Hongladarom 2002, 241, 243).

Negroponte (1995, 193) points out that the computer, and especially electronic mail, has changed people's availability. Twenty-four-hour television news networks such as CNN caused the institution of the nine o'clock news to lose its significance. This was even more the case with the advent of Internet news, available everywhere all the time, no matter what time zone the audience was in. As Lee and Liebenau (2000, 52) observe, the Internet is always 'on" and provides constant news flows.

Internet news time is different from other news times because days and hours are no longer marked by the news as they were on radio and television. News is available on the Internet all the time and the user can start reading it at any time. As one young woman said, "Waiting for the evening TV news would seem like going back to the dark ages. News fits around you now" (Hargreaves and Thomas 2002, 52).

News has become timeless because it is available all the time. Hence it loses its previous value, which was based on its scarcity. Even if a particular piece of news is the first report of a particular event, it is followed in no time at all by other reports. As a result, news is at the same time everywhere and nowhere. As one young man said, "news grabs you more than you grab it" (Hargreaves and Thomas 2002, 44).

The hypertextual nature of Internet news makes its time multi-layered. The news is linked to so much other news that its timing keeps changing as it is updated. This kind of news follows its own time, no matter in which time zones it is originated and consumed. Although news is still dated and timed, the time keeps changing with updating, and is never still in the way it was when printed news was first available. A reader of printed news could always see the difference between the time the news was sent and the time at which she was reading it. With Internet news, the times of both dispatch and receipt keep moving simultaneously. There is no precise moment. Unlike broadcast news, where time is not visible in the news itself, the Internet adds its own time to the very screen on which the news is shown.

Hypertextuality also changes the relationship between events and news. With computers the transmission time between events and the news of those events shrinks and often event and news become simultaneous. However, there is an even wider application: the difference between news and events disappears when news becomes an event and events become news. Hypertextuality in news is a continuous linking between the different sites of news and of events, and in the end it is hard to tell what is an event and what is news.

With the Internet, news has become available all the time. People do not have to wait for news, because news is everywhere even when one travels. News has stopped being a marker of time, because the flow of news is constant. Inside news, time does not matter in the same way as it mattered before: every story is almost in real time and the link between source, event, and time no longer needs to be constructed linearly. News is linked to other news and this network of news constantly updates itself without a need to specify its source

Tomorrow

News can never really be defined as anything other than information, which is new and of interest to other people, but today people have a very large number of ways to inform themselves. (Hargreaves 2000, 60)

There are two issues here. First, news is everywhere. Because it is everywhere, it has lost part of its former value. Nobody wants to pay for a general news service, but everybody wants to use it. Second, the traditional division between wholesalers and retailers, in which news agencies were wholesalers of news to the media, has become outdated since news is provided and consumed by almost everyone. As a result it is difficult to define news. News could be anything from news stories to new stories, information and comments, or possibly all these categories at once.

Scholars, news reporters, and audiences have equally been influenced by news that we recognize as news. This is a nineteenth-century concept of news, but everybody thinks they know what news is. It is no coincidence that the media everywhere now ask their audience to give or sell them news. The expectation is that even audiences now know what news is and can "find" it. However, if audiences become newsgatherers, where does this leave journalists? Previously only journalists were trained and thus qualified to "find" and "edit" "objective" news, but what is their new role in this new situation where they ask their audiences to give them news? Everybody is now news-literate to the extent to which professional journalists, as we have defined them since the nineteenth century, are opening their ranks to everybody. As Lowery (2006, 479) observes, the process of newsgathering is a rarity for bloggers, but is routine for journalists. No type of online news is primarily concerned with the collection of news – it simply relies on traditional newsgatherers.

We need to think seriously about how we define news. If it is no longer the nineteenth-century concept of the newness and objectivity of news, what is it? If the difference, for example, between news and comment is disappearing, as it does in blogging, where does this leave news that only relies on "facts"? Is there a new quest for intelligent and informative commentators on news? Or do we all rely on information, no matter where it comes from, and form our own opinions?

New media and communications technology expand the possibilities: it is up to individuals and groups to achieve access to this technology if it is not available. Perhaps this is the struggle of the Information Age: no longer a question of taking over the means of production, as in the Industrial Age, but of taking over the means of media and communication technology. But what is the most important content: information or news?

I see at least four developments taking place. First, the difference between events and news is disappearing. Second, the difference between information and news is disappearing. Third, the difference between news and comment is disappearing. Fourth, the difference between news and entertainment is disappearing. All of these will change the nature of news as we know it.

It is no longer new for events to be increasingly orchestrated, especially public events. For example, in the UK the Labour government hired "spin doctors" to inform and guide journalists about what it considers important. In 2000 it was estimated that the Government Information and Communications Service employed around 1,200 information officers, plus support staff, and had a budget running into hundreds of millions of pounds (Miller and Dinan, 2000: 11). In 2006 this had increased to 1,815 press officers and public relations staff in the main departments across Whitehall and a further 1,444 working for the 200 quangos and agencies funded by taxpayers. As a result, we can talk about the fifth estate, a new professional group of public relations specialists who know how to make news (Perry 2007). Many of these have previously worked as journalists and thus have experience of working "on both sides of the fence." As a result, most political events are "newsed," even before they become news. Journalists often work on pre-fabricated materials that have already been written up in a form ready for easy use.

Second, because of this decreasing difference between events and news and of the advent of citizen journalism, it is increasingly difficult to tell the difference between news and information. Those who sell news and want to make a profit must emphasize that their product is news rather than information. If it is labeled information, it must be information that is exclusive, trustworthy, and timely and that is not available free anywhere else. It is more and more difficult to make a profit from general news services because this information/news is available everywhere all the time. But even the "old" media such as newspapers have increased their output of news. In many big cities news is now given free to anybody who bothers to pick up a freesheet on his or her way to or from work. This is one example of the overproduction of news.

One of the solutions is to offer tailored news. This may be a special kind of news, for example financial news. It may be news addressed to a special group of people, such as a minority language group. The problem with this scenario concerns the general public and its rights to be informed. We are not necessarily so far away from a time when those with power could afford their own private news service while the masses were dependent on a modern version of the medieval "new stories."

The third difference that is disappearing is that between news and comment. News has never been completely "objective," but it has always been mainly factual. Increasingly, citizen journalism, especially blogging, mixes news and comment. It does not claim to be impartial; on the contrary, it openly confesses its biased view. This of course contrasts with most news media, which claim to be "objective" and "impartial" even if they are not. When there is an information/news overflow there is a need for enlightened and informed comment.

The fourth difference that is disappearing is that between news and entertainment. This not only means that news now increasingly covers non-hard news topics, but also affects the ways news is presented. Increasingly, news presenters want to sound and look more informal, to chat about the news. Recently, Yahoo actually announced that it would hire a news singer. "This project will create an entirely new kind of news beat, so stay tuned," a company spokesperson said. "All I can say for now is that this reporter will leave you tapping your feet" (Wallenstein 2007).

The consumption of news is thus made as easy as possible. We have access to news on the bus, at the station, in the Internet café. News has become very ordinary. The difference between news and other genres is no longer always clear. Where news has become soft, the boundaries between news and entertainment have become blurred.

Yesterday Was Today

Let me finish with three different examples.

Example 1

Between 1500 and 1800, hawkers, charlatans, and ballad-mongers were performing *new stories* on street corners, right next to bear-wards, buffoons, clowns, comedians, and hocus-pocus men (Burke 1994, 94–95). These new stories were not necessarily new and did not look like what we now know as news, but they had elements that later became recognized as characteristics of the news genre. Little difference was then perceived between novels and news, between facts and fiction. Personal letters were also considered to be new stories, and as such were shared with other people. New stories were exchanged both within and between cities whose communication networks were crucial to their status.

Example 2

More than 140 years ago, Messrs Havas, Wolff, and Reuter met in Paris, on July 15, 1859, to discuss their new business, the sale of electronically transmitted news. They had all founded *telegraph agencies* which bore their own names and now they joined in signing their first exclusive contract with one another, dividing the global electronic news market between them. Some 90 years later, on February 13, 1934 in New York, Sir Roderick Jones of Reuters news agency met Mr Kent Cooper of the Associated Press. When Cooper informed him that the AP did not want to sign a contract with Reuters, Sir Roderick said: "Mr Cooper, I need to have a contract. Whatever contract you draw up I will sign." They eventually signed a contract which would end the exclusive exchange of global news established in 1859.[10]

Example 3

The postmodern blog evolved from online diaries where people keep a running account (or blog) of their personal lives. As with the new stories of the Middle Ages, modern bloggers "sing" their stories, next to other performers, not on the street corner but on the World Wide Web. Nothing needs to "travel" any more: not news, nor journalists, nor individuals; they all meet virtually on the World Wide Web. The era of "pure" news is over: almost everybody who has access to technology can now become a news reporter or commentator.

What happened between the first example and the third example? In the first, we have individual news-mongers selling their songs on street corners in their respective cities, singing to an audience of very limited size. In the second, we see the first emerging global news companies selling their news to the media and establishing their exclusive markets. This gave rise to a rapidly increasing audience of millions and millions of people scattered around the world, first reading their news in newspapers and then listening to it on the radio or watching it on television, mainly at home, but also when they were traveling and were able to carry their newspaper or radio with them on their way to work or play. In the third example, as the BBC Director of Global News put it, "News organizations do not own the news any more" (Sambrook 2006). The audience is no longer performing a simultaneous act of reading the same paper at the same time, listening to the same news broadcast or even watching the same television news. Instead, they are traveling virtually to somewhere on the net and reading/ watching the news whenever they find it convenient. Mass audiences have been broken down again into individuals standing on virtual highways – this time not with a group, but alone and ready to move on.

Throughout my book I have argued that we need to study not only the modernization of news, but its historical development through media and communications as far back as the Middle Ages. Considering the historical trajectory of news from news hawkers in the Middle Ages to bloggers in the Information Age, it is possible to argue that we are now witnessing the death of "modern" news, as conceived in the nineteenth century. In this situation of multiple change, serious thought is required about what constitutes news. Everybody thinks they know what news is, but in fact nobody can define the twenty-first-century concept of news. The boundaries are again becoming blurred. News may again become just new stories.

Notes

1   www.bbc.co.uk/commissioning/marketresearch/audiencegroup5.shtml, accessed October 27, 2008.
2   www.turismocastillayleon.com/cm/turcyl/tkContent?pgseed=1186761552562 &idContent=8650&locale=es_ES&textOnly=false, accessed October 27, 2008.
3   www.bbc.co.uk/commissioning/marketresearch/audiencegroup2.shtml, accessed October 27, 2008.
4   *News Audiences Increasingly Politicized. Online News Audience Larger, More Diverse* (2004). The Pew Research Center for The People and The Press Report. Available at http://people-press.org/reports/display.php3?PageID=833, accessed May 22, 2008.
5   *Internet news audience highly critical of news organizations. views of press values and performance: 1985–2007* (2007). The Pew Research Center for The People and The Press Report. Available at http://people-press.org/reports/display. php3?ReportID=348, accessed May 22, 2008.
6   http://news.google.co.uk/nwshp?hl=en&ned=uk, accessed October 27, 2008.
7   http://people-press.org/reports/display.php3?ReportID=36, accessed October 27, 2008.
8   www.stateofthenewsmedia.org/2008/narrative_online_citizen_media. php?cat=6&media=5, accessed October 27, 2008.
9   Ibid.
10 A letter from W. Turner to Mr Moloney on May 23, 1935. Sir Roderick Jones papers, Section 2, Box file 2. Reuters' archive.

Bibliography

Anderson, B. (1991) *Imagined Communities: Reflections on the Origin and Spread of Nationalism*. Verso, London.

Appadurai, A. (1990) Disjuncture and difference in the global cultural economy. *Public Culture* 2(3), 1–23.

Archer, G.L. (1938) *The History of Radio to 1926*. The American Historical Society, New York.

Augé, M. (1995) *Non-Places: Introduction to an Anthropology of Supermodernity*. Verso, London.

Baldasty, G.J. (1992) *The Commercialization of News in the 19th Century*. University of Wisconsin Press, Madison.

Barker, H. (2000) *Newspapers, Politics and English Society*. Longman, Edinburgh.

Basse, D. (1991) *Wolff's Telegaphisches Bureau 1849 bis 1933. Agenturpublizistik zwischen Politik und Wirtschaft*. Kommunikation und Politik 21. K.G. Saur, Munich.

Bauman, Z. (2000) *Liquid Modernity*. Polity, Cambridge.

BBC Commissioning (2006) Available online at www.bbc.co.uk/commissioning/marketresearch/audiencegroup5.shtml. Accessed October 27, 2008.

Beale, P.O. (2005) *England's Mail. Two Millennia of Letter Writing*. Tempus Publishing, Stroud.

Beck, U. (2000) *What is Globalization?* Polity Press, Cambridge.

Beck, U. (2002) The cosmopolitan society and its enemies. *Theory, Culture and Society* 20(19), 17–44.

Bell, A. (1991) *The Language of News Media*. Blackwell, Oxford.

Benét, V. (1933) The United Press. *Fortune*, May, 67–104.

Best, S.J., Chmielewski, B., and Krueger, B.S. (2005) Selective exposure to online foreign news during the conflict with Iraq. *Harvard International Journal of Press/Politics* 10(4), 52–70.

Beynon, J. and Dunkerley, D. (eds) (2000) *Globalization. The Reader*. The Athlone Press, London.

Billig, M. (1995) *Banal Nationalism*. Sage, London.

Black, J. (2001) *The English Press 1621–1861*. Sutton Publishing, Stroud.

Blanchard, M.A. (1987) The Associated Press antitrust suit: a philosophical clash over ownership of First Amendment rights. *Business History Review* 61(1): 43–85.

Blondheim, M. (1994) *News Over the Wires: The Telegraph and the Flow of Public Information in America, 1844–1897*. Harvard University Press, Cambridge, MA.

Boczkowski, P. (2004) *Digitizing the News. Innovation in Online Newspapers*. MIT Press, Cambridge, MA.

Bolter, J.D. (1984) *Turing's Man*. University of North Carolina Press, Chapel Hill.

Bolter, J.D. (1991) *Writing Space. The Computer, Hypertext, and the History of Writing*. Lawrence Erlbaum Associates, Hillsdale, NJ.

Boyd-Barrett, O. (1980) *The International News Agencies*. Constable. London.

Boyd-Barrett, O. (1986) News agencies. Political constraints and market opportunities: the case of the "Big Four." In: Kivikuru, U. and Varis, T. (eds) *Textbook on Approaches to International Communication: Textbook for Journalism Education*. Finnish National Commission for UNESCO, No 68, Helsinki, 67–93.

Boyd-Barrett, O. (1998) "Global" news agencies: Trends and issues over 150 years. In Boyd-Barrett, O. and Rantanen, T. (eds) *The Globalization of News*. Sage, London, 19–34.

Boyd-Barrett, O. (2000) Constructing the global, constructing the local. In: Malek, A. and Kavoori, A.P. (eds) *The Global Dynamics of News*. Ablex, Stamford, CT, 299–321.

Brake, D. (2008) A private interview on the Internet. London, May 20.

Braudel, F. (1979/1984) *The Perspective of the World* [*Le temps du monde*], trans. Siân Reynolds. Collins, London.

Briggs, A. and Burke, P. (2005) *A Social History of the Media: from Gutenberg to the Internet*. 2nd edn, Polity Press, Cambridge.

Brown, L. (1985) *Victorian News and Newspapers*. Clarendon Press, Oxford.

Bücher, K. (1908) *Die Entstehung der Volkswirtschaft*. H. Laupp, Tübingen.

Bücher , K. (1915) *Unsere Sache und die Tagespresse*. J.C.B. Mohr (P. Siebeck), Tübingen.

Burke, P. (1994) *Popular Culture in Early Modern Europe*. Revised reprint. Scolar Press, Aldershot.

Carey, J.W. (1989) *Communication as Culture. Essays on Media and Society*. Unwin Hyman, Boston, MA.

Carey, J.W. (1998) The Internet and the end of the national communication system: uncertain predictions of an uncertain future. *Journalism and Mass Communication Quarterly* 75(1), 28–34.

Carlson, M. (2007) Order versus access: news search engines and the challenge to traditional journalistic roles. *Media, Culture and Society* 29(6), 1014–1030.

Castells, M. (1989) *The Informational City. Information Technology, Economic Restructuring, and the Urban-Regional Process.* Blackwell, Oxford.

Castells, M. (1996) *The Rise of the Network Society.* Blackwell, Oxford.

Certeau de, M. (1984) *The Practice of Everyday Life.* University of California Press, Berkeley.

Chalaby, J.K. (1996) Journalism as an Anglo-American invention. *European Journal of Communication* 11(3), 303–326.

Chalaby, J.K. (1998) *The Invention of Journalism.* Macmillan Press, Basingstoke.

Chalaby, J.K. (2005) From internationalization to transnationalization. *Global Media and Communication* 1(1), 28–32.

Cherry, C. (1977) The telephone system: creator of mobility and social change. In: De Sola Pool, I. (ed.) *The Social Impact of the Telephone.* MIT Press, Cambridge, MA, 112–127.

Chyi, H.I. and Sylvie, G. (2001) The medium is global, the content is not: the role of geography in online newspaper markets. *Journal of Media Economics* 14(4), 231–248.

Clanchy, M.T. (1979/1994) *From Memory to Written Record. England 1066–1307.* Blackwell, Oxford.

Cooper, K. (1942) *Barriers Down. The Story of the News Agency Epoch.* J.J. Little and Ives Company, New York.

Cowling, J. (2005) Digital news: genie's lamp or Pandora's box? Paper given at IPPR Seminar *News and Information: Where Next? The Professionals' View.* London, May 27, 2005.

Crang, M. (1998) *Cultural Geography.* Routledge, London.

Creel, G. (1920) *How We Advertised America. The First Telling of the Amazing Story of the Committee on Public Information that Carried the Gospel of Americanism to Every Corner of the Globe.* Harper and Brothers, New York.

Cuthbert, M. (1980) Reaction to international news agencies: 1930s and 1970s compared. *Gazette* 42(26), 99–110.

Czitrom, D.J. (1982) *Media and the American Mind. From Morse to McLuhan.* University of North Carolina Press, Chapel Hill.

Darnton, R. (1995) *The Forbidden Best-Sellers of Pre-Revolutionary France.* W.W. Norton and Company, New York.

Darnton, R. (2000) An early information society: news and the media in eighteenth-century Paris. *The American Historical Review,* 105(1), 1–35.

Davis, L.J. (1980) A social history of fact and fiction: authorial disavowal in the early English novel. In: Said, E.D. (ed.) *Literature and Society.* Johns Hopkins University Press, Baltimore, MD, 120–148.

Davis, L.J. (1983) *Factual Fictions. The Origins of the English Novel.* University of Pennsylvania Press, Philadelphia.

Desmond, R.W. (1937) *The Press and World Affairs.* D. Appleton-Century Company, New York.

Deuze, M. (2003) The Web and its journalism: considering the consequences of different types of new media online. *New Media and Society* 5(2), 203–230.

Dörfler, E. and Pensold, W. (2001) *Die Macht der Nachricht. Die Geschichte der Nachrichtenagenturen in Österreich.* Molden Verlag, Vienna.

Dreyfus, H.L. (1995) *Being-in-the-World. A Commentary on Heidegger's* Being and Time, *division I.* MIT Press, Cambridge, MA.

Du Boff, R.B. (1984) The rise of communications regulation: the telegraph industry. *Journal of Communication* 34(3), 52–66.

Eisenstein, E.L. (1979/2005) *The Printing Revolution in Early Modern Europe.* 2nd edn. Cambridge University Press, Cambridge.

Eisenstein, E.L. (1997) *The Printing Press as an Agent of Change. Communications and Cultural Transformations in Early-Modern Europe.* Cambridge University Press, Cambridge.

Elliot, P.and Golding, P. (1974) Mass communication and social change. In: De Kadt, E. and Williams, K. (eds) *Sociology and Development.* Tavistock, London, 229–254.

Encyclopaedia Britannica (1911a) Newspapers. 11th edition, Vol. XIX. Cambridge University Press, Cambridge, 544–581.

Encyclopaedia Britannica (1911b) "Telegraph," 11th edition, Vol. XXVI. Cambridge, Cambridge University Press, 510–540.

Entrikin, J.N. (1991) *The Betweenness of Place. Towards a Geography of Modernity.* Johns Hopkins University Press, Baltimore, MD.

Ferguson, M. (1990) Electronic media and the redefining of time and space. In: Ferguson, M. (ed.) *Public Communication. The New Imperatives. Future Directions for Media Research.* Sage, London, 152–172.

Feuilherade, P. (2004) Online newspapers tempt readers. Available online at http://news.bbc.co.uk/1/hi/technology/3767267.stm, accessed May 22, 2008.

Fields, G. (2004) *Territories of Profit: Communications, Capitalist Development, and Innovation at G.F. Swift and Dell Computer.* Stanford Business Books, Stanford, CA.

The Flow of News (1953) The International Press Institute, Zurich.

Fourth Pacific Science Congress (1929). Batavia-Bandoeng (Java), May–June. Historical review of the development of the telegraph-telephone and radio services in the Pacific by the post-telegraph and telephone service in the Netherlands Indies. N.V. Drukkeru Maks and V.S. Klits, Bandoeng.

Frédérix, P. (1959) *Un siècle de chasse aux nouvelles: de l'agence d'information Havas à l'Agence France-Presse.* Flammarion, Paris.

Fuchs, F. (1919) *Telegraphische Nachrichtenbüros.* Dietrich Reimer, Berlin.

Galtung, J. and Ruge, M. H. (1965) The structure of foreign news. the presentation of the Congo, Cuba and Cyprus crises in four Norwegian newspapers. *Journal of Peace Research* 2(1), 64–91.

Gans, H. (1979) *Deciding What's News.* Pantheon, New York.

Garnham, N. (1994) *Capitalism and Communication: Global Culture and the Economics of Information.* Sage, London.

Giddens, A. (1990) *The Consequences of Modernity.* Polity Press, Cambridge.

Gillespie, A. and Robins, R. (1989) Geographical inequalities: the spatial bias of the news communications technologies. *Journal of Communication* 39(3), 7–18.

Gitlin, T. (2003) *The Whole World is Watching. Mass Media in the Making and Unmaking of the New Left.* University of California Press, Berkeley.

Gramling, O.(1940) *AP: The Story of the News.* Farrar and Rinehart, Inc., New York.

Groth, O. (1928) *Die Zeitung.* J. Bensheimer, Mannheim.

Gurevich, A.J. (1972) *Categories of Medieval Culture.* Routledge and Kegan Paul, London.

Habermas, J. (1989) *The Structural Transformation of the Public Sphere: An Inquiry into a Category of Bourgeois Society.* Polity Press, Oxford.

Hachtmann, R. (2001) The European capital cities in the revolution of 1848. In: Dowe, D., Haupt, H.-G., Langewiesche, D., and Sperber, J. (eds) *Europe in 1848. Revolution and Reform*, trans. David Higgins. Berghahn Books, New York, 341–370.

A Half Century of Cable Service to The Three Americas, 1878–1928. All America Cables Inc, New York.

Hallin, D.C. (1986) Where? Cartography, community, and the cold war. In: Manoff, R.K. and Schudson, M. (eds) *Reading the News.* Pantheon Books, New York, 109–145.

Hannerz, U. (1996) *Transnational Connections: Culture, People, Places.* Routledge, London.

Hargreaves, I. (2000) Is there a future for foreign news? *Historical Journal of Film, Radio and Television* 20(1), 55–61.

Hargreaves, I. and Thomas, J. (2002) *New News, Old News.* Broadcasting Standards Commission, London.

Harris, M. (1978) 1620–1780. In: Boyce, G., Curran, J., and Wingate, P. (eds) *Newspaper History: from the 17th Century to the Present Day.* Constable, London, 82–97.

Harris, M. (1990) A few shillings for small books: the experiences of a flying stationer in the 18th century. In: Myers, R. and Harris, M. (eds) *Spreading the Word: The Distribution Networks of Print 1550–1850.* St Paul's Bibliographies, Winchester, 83–108.

Harris, P. (1977) News dependence: the case for a new world information order. Unpublished final report to the United Nations Educational, Scientific, and Cultural Organization of a study of the international news media.

Hart, J.A. (1970) *The Developing Views on the News Editorial Syndrome 1500–1800.* Southern Illinois University Press, Carbondale, IL.

Harvey, D. (1989) *The Condition of Postmodernity: An Enquiry into the Origins of Cultural Change.* Blackwell, Oxford.

Harvey, D. (1993) From space to place and back again: reflections on the condition of postmodernity. In: Bird, J., Curtis, B., Putnam, T., and Tickner, L. (eds) *Mapping the Futures. Local Culture, Global Change.* Routledge, London, 3–29.

Haupt, H.-G. and Langewiesche, D. (2001) The European revolution of 1848. Its political and social reforms, its politics of nationalism, and its short- and long-term consequences. In: Dowe, D., Haupt, H.-G., Langewiesche, D., and Sperber, J. (eds) *Europe in 1848. Revolution and Reform,* trans. David Higgins. Berghahn Books, New York, 1–24.

Headrick, D.R. (1991) *The Invisible Weapon: Telecommunications and International Politics 1851–1945.* Oxford University Press, Oxford.

Heidegger, M. (1995) *Being and Time.* Blackwell, Oxford.

Heimbürger, H. (1938) *Svenska telegraphverket. Det statliga telefonväsendet 1881– 1902 Televerket,* Vol. 1. Stockholm.

Hesmondhalgh, D. (2002) *The Cultural Industries.* Sage, London.

Hindman, M., Tsioutsiouliklis, K., and Johnson, J.A. (2003) Googlearchy: how a few heavily linked sites dominate politics online. Paper presented at the annual meeting of the Midwest Political Science Association. Available online at www.johnkeane.net/pdf_docs/teaching_sources/google/google.pdf, accessed November 1, 2008.

Hobsbawm, E. (1975) *The Age of Capital 1848–1875.* Weidenfeld and Nicolson, London.

Hohenberg, J. (1973) *Free Press, Free People: The Best Cause.* Free Press, New York.

Höhne, H.(1977) *Report über Nachrichtenagenturen 2. Die Geschichte der Nachricht und ihrer Verbreiter.* Nomos Verlagsgesellschaft, Baden-Baden.

Hongladarom, S. (2002) The web of time and the dilemma of globalization. *The Information Society* 18(1), 241–249.

Hönig, E.A. (1998) *Printing and the Market in Early Modern Antwerp.* Yale University Press, New Haven, CT.

Hoskins, C., McFadyen, S., and Finn, A. (1997) *Global Television and Film. An Introduction to the Economics of the Business.* Clarendon Press, Oxford.

Hoskins, C., McFadyen, S., and Finn, A. (2004) *Media Economics. Applying Economics to New and Traditional Media.* Sage, Thousand Oaks, CA.

Höyer, S. (2003) Newspapers without journalists. *Journalism Studies* 4(4), 451–463.

Hunter, J.P. (1989) News and new things. In: Desan, P., Parkhurst Ferguson, P., and Griswold, W. (eds) *Literature and Social Practice.* University of Chicago Press, Chicago, 114–136.

Hunter, J.P. (1990) *Before Novels. The Cultural Contexts of Eighteenth-Century English Fiction.* W.E. Norton and Company, New York.

Ingmar, G. (1973) *Monopol på nyheter. Ekonomiska och politiska aspekter på svenska och internationella nyhetsbyråers verksamhet 1870–1919.* Esselte Studium, Uppsala.

Innis, H. (1950/1972) *Empire and Communication.* University of Toronto Press, Toronto.

Kahn, A.E. (1968) Cartels and trade associations. In: Sills, D.L. (ed.) *International Encyclopedia of the Social Sciences.* Macmillan, New York, 320–325.

Kern, S. (1983) *The Culture of Time and Space 1880–1918.* Harvard University Press, Cambridge, MA.

Kiss, J. (2008) Newspaper ABCs. Soaring online user figures offer solace – and challenges. Available online at www.guardian.co.uk/media/2008/feb/25/pressandpublishing.abcs, accessed May 22, 2008.

Koch, U.F. (2001) Power and impotence of the press in 1848: France and Germany in comparison. In: Dowe, D., Haupt, H.-G., Langewiesche, D., and Sperber, J. (eds) *Europe in 1848. Revolution and Reform,* trans. David Higgins. Berghahn Book, New York, 559–584.

Lash, S. and J. Urry (1994) *Economies of Signs and Space.* Sage, London.

Lee, H. and Liebenau, J. (2000) Time and the Internet at the turn of the millennium. *Time and Society* 9(1), 43–56.

Lee, H. and Whitley, E.A. (1999) Time and information technology: monochronicity, polychronity and temporal symmetry. *European Journal of Information Systems* 8(1), 16–26.

Lefebvre, H. (1991) *The Production of Space.* Blackwell, Oxford.

Le Goff, J. (1980) *Time, Work and Culture in the Middle Ages.* University of Chicago Press, Chicago.

Lenhart, A. and Fox, S. (2006) Bloggers: A portrait of the Internet's new storytellers. A Pew Research Center for The People and The Press Report. Available online at www.pewinternet.org/PPF/r/186/report_display.asp, accessed May 22, 2008.

Lowe, D.M. (1982) *History of Bourgeois Perception.* University of Chicago Press, Chicago.

Lowery, W. (2006) Mapping the journalism–blogging relationship. *Journalism* 7(4), 477–500.

MacBride, S. (1980) *Many Voices, One World: Towards a New and More Efficient Information and Communication Order.* Kogan Page, London.

Matheson, D. (2004) Weblogs and the epistemology of the news: some trends in online journalism. *New Media and Society* 6(4), 443–468.

Mattelart, A. (2000) *Networking the World 1794–2000.* University of Minnesota Press, Minneapolis.

McCarthy, C. (2006) Google reveals payment deal with AP. Available online at http://news.zdnet.com/2100-9588_22-6102109.html, accessed May 22, 2008.

McClatchy, V.S. (1919) *Statement*. Hearings before the Subcommittee on the Merchant Marine and Fisheries. House of Representatives. 66th Congress, 1st Session. Government Printing Office, Washington, DC, 4–21.

McIntosh, S. (2005) Web review: blogs: has their time finally come – or gone? *Global Media and Communication* 1(4), 385–388.

McNeill, J.R. and McNeill, W.H. (2003) *The Human Web. A Bird's Eye View of World History.* W.W. Norton and Company, New York.

Meyrowitz, J. (1985) *No Sense of Place: The Impact of Electronic Media on Social Behaviour.* Oxford University Press, Oxford.

Morley, D. and Robins, K. (1995) *Spaces of Identity: Global Media, Electronic Landscapes and Cultural Boundaries.* Routledge, London.

Morris, J. (2008) A personal interview on blogging. London, May 15.

Mumford, L. (1934) *Technics and Civilization.* Harcourt, Brace, and Co, New York.

Naujoks E. (1963) Bismarck und das Wolffsche Telegraphenbüro. *Geschichte in Wissenschaft und Unterricht,* 14(22), 605–616.

Negroponte, N. (1995) *Being Digital.* Vintage Books, New York.

Nerone, J. and Barnhurst, K.(2001) *The Form of News: a History.* Guilford Press, New York and London.

Nicholas, D. (2003) *Urban Europe, 1100–1700.* Palgrave Macmillan, Basingstoke.

Nowotny, H. (1994) *Time: Modern and Postmodern Experience,* trans. N. Plaice. Polity Press, Oxford, Cambridge.

Oates, J. (2005) AFP sues Google. Agence France Presse is suing Google for linking to its news stories. Available online at www.theregister.co.uk/2005/03/21/afp_sues_google/, accessed May 22, 2008.

Ong, W.J. (1982) *Orality and Literacy. The Technologizing of the World.* Routledge, London.

Palmer, M. (1976) L'agence Havas et Bismarck. L'echec de la Triple Alliance Télégraphique (1887–1889). *Revue d'histoire diplomatique* July/December, 321–357.

Palser, B. (2002) Journalistic blogging. *American Journalism Review* July/August. Available online at www.ajr.org/article.asp?id=2571, accessed May 22, 2008.

Park, R.E. (1922) *The Immigrant Press and Its Control.* Harper and Brothers, New York.

Park, R.E., Burgess, E.W., and McKenzie, R.D. (1967) *The City.* University of Chicago Press, Chicago.

Paterson, C. (2006) News Agency Dominance in International News on the Internet. Papers in International and Global Communication No. 01/06. Centre for International Communications Research, Leeds University. Available online at http://ics.leeds.ac.uk/papers/cicr/exhibits/42/cicrpaterson.pdf, accessed May 22, 2008.

Pennanen, S. (2007) Lapset uutisten katsojina – 5-6 vuotiaiden käsityksiä ja kokemuksia uutisista.[5- to 6-year-old children's impressions and experiences on TV news]. *Tiedotustutkimus* 30(2), 17–31.

Pentikäinen, J.Y. (1989) *Kalevala Mythology*, trans. and ed. Ritva Poom. Indiana University Press, Bloomington.

Perry, J. (2007) Whose news: Who is the political news gatekeeper in the early 21st century? Unpublished PhD dissertation. Department of Media and Communications. London School of Economics and Political Science.

Philips, P. (2007) New news future news. Available online at www.ofcom.org.uk/media/speeches/2007/07/nnfn, accessed May 22, 2008.

Potter, S.J. (2003) *News and the British World. The Emergence of an Imperial Press System, 1876–1922*. Clarendon Press, Oxford.

Putnis, P. (2002) New Media Regulation: The Case of Copyright in Telegraphic News in Australia, 1869–1912. Paper prepared for Communications Research Forum, Canberra, October 2002.

Quah, D. (2003) *The Weightless Economy*, available online at http://econ.lse.ac.uk/~dquah/tweirl0.html, accessed July 26, 2004.

The Radio Industry. The Story of its Development (1928) A.W. Shaw Company, Chicago.

Rantanen, T. (1987) 'STT:n uutisia' sadan vuoden varrelta. Weilin & Göös, Espoo.

Rantanen, T. (1990) *Foreign News in Imperial Russia: The Relationship between International and Russian News Agencies, 1856–1914*. Federation of Finnish Scientific Societies, Helsinki.

Rantanen, T. (1992) *Mr Howard Goes to South America: The United Press Associations and Foreign Expansion*. Roy W. Howard Monographs in Journalism and Mass Communication Research, 2. School of Journalism, Indiana University, Bloomington.

Rantanen, T. (1994) *Howard Interviews Stalin. How the AP, UP and TASS Smashed the International News Cartel*. Roy W. Howard Monographs in Journalism and Mass Communication Research, 3. School of Journalism, Indiana University, Bloomington.

Rantanen, T. (1997) The Globalisation of News in the 19th Century. *Media Culture and Society* 19(4), 605–620.

Rantanen, T. (1998) *After Five O'Clock Friends. Kent Cooper and Roy W. Howard*. Roy H. Howard Monographs in Journalism and Mass Communication Research, 4. School of Journalism, Indiana University, Bloomington.

Rantanen, T. (2002) *The Global and the National. Media and Communications in Post-Communist Russia*. Rowman and Littlefield, Lanham, MD.

Rantanen, T. (2005) Cosmopolitanization Now! An interview with Ulrich Beck. *Global Media and Communication* 1(3), 247–263.

Rantanen, T. (2006a) Flows and contra-flows in transitional societies. Russia and China compared, In: Thussu, D.K. (ed.) *The Global Media Bazaar: Contra-Flow in Cultural Products.* Routledge, London, 165–181.

Rantanen, T. (2006b) News agencies. their structure and operation revisited. Paper presented at the EANA Conference in Geneva, September.

Rantanen, T. and Boyd-Barrett, O. (2001) State news agencies – a time for re-evaluation? *Medien und Zeit,* 16(4), 38–45.

Read, D. (1994) Reuters: news agency of the British Empire. *Contemporary Record* 8(2), 195–212.

Read, D. (1999) *The Power of News.* Oxford University Press, Oxford.

Reese, S.D., Rutigliano, L., Hyun, K., and Jeong, J. (2007) Mapping the blogosphere: Professional and citizen-based media in the global news arena. *Journalism* 8(3), 235–261.

Reitz, J. (1991) Das Deutsche Nachrichtenbüro. In: Wilke, J. (ed.) *Telegraphenbüros und Nachrictenagenturen in Deutschland. Untersuchungen zu ihrer Geschichte bis 1949.* K.G. Saur, Munich, 213–264.

Relph, E. (1976) *Place and Placelessness.* Pion, London.

Rifkin, J. (1987) *Time Wars: The Primary Conflict in Human History.* H. Holt, New York.

Rings, J. (1936) *Amerikanische Nachrichtenagenturen.* Drück der Limburger Vereinsdrückerei, Berlin.

Robertson. R. (1992) *Globalization: Social Theory and Global Culture.* Sage, London.

Rogers, W.S. (1919a) Statement. Hearing before a Subcommittee on Naval Affairs. US Senate. 66th Congress. First session on the government ownership or control of radiotelegraphy and cable communication in its military and commercial aspects, In: *Use of Naval Stations for Commercial Purposes.* Part 1. Government Printing Office, Washington, DC, 2–20.

Rogers, W.S. (1919b) Testimony. Hearing before the Committee on Foreign Affairs. House of Representatives. 66th Congress, first session on H.R. 9822. In: *Use of Naval Stations for Commercial Purposes.* Government Printing Office, Washington, DC, 103–118.

Roschko, B. (1975) *Newsmaking.* University of Chicago Press, Chicago.

Rosewater, V. (1930) *History of Cooperative News-gathering in the United States.* D. Appleton and Company, New York.

Rowbotham, S. (2000) *Promise of a Dream.* Penguin Press, London.

Sack, D. (1992) *Place, Modernity, and the Consumer's World.* Johns Hopkins University Press, Baltimore, MD.

Sambrook, R. (2006) How the net is transforming news. Available online at http://news.bbc.co.uk/1/hi/technology/4630890.stm, accessed May 24, 2008.

Sandbothe, M. (1997) *The Transversal Logic of the World Wide Web. A Philosophical Analysis.* Paper given at the 11th Annual Computers and Philosophy

Conference in Pittsburgh (PA). Available online at www.sandbothe.net, accessed May 22, 2008.

Sandbothe, M. (1998) The temporalization of time in modern philosophy. In: Baert, P. (ed.) *Time in Modern Intellectual Thought*. Elsevier, Amsterdam. Available online at www.sandbothe.net, accessed May 22, 2008.

Sandbothe, M. (1999) Media temporalities of the Internet: philosophies of time and media in Derrida and Rorty. *AI and Society* 13(4), 421–434.

Sarnoff, D. (1928) *The Development of the Radio Art and Radio Industry since 1920*. A lecture delivered before the Harvard Business School, April 16, 1928, Boston.

Sassen, S. (1991/2001) *The Global City*. Princeton University Press, Princeton, NJ.

Sassen, S. (1994/2006) *Cities in a World Economy*. Pine Forge Press, Thousand Oaks, CA.

Sassen, S. (1996) *Losing Control*. Columbia University Press, New York.

Sassen, S. (2004) Local actors in global politics. *Current Sociology* 52(4), 649–670

Scannell, P. (1996) *Radio, Television and Modern Life. A Phenomenological Approach*. Blackwell, Oxford.

Schivelbusch, W. (1978) Railroad space and railroad time. *New German Critique* 5(14), 31–40.

Schlesinger, P.R. (1995) *Europeanisation and the Media: National Identity and the Public Sphere*, Arena Working Paper, 7. Norwegian Research Council, Oslo.

Schudson, M. (1978) *Discovering the News: A Social History of American Newspapers*. Basic Books, New York.

Schudson, M. (1995) *The Power of News*. Harvard University Press, Cambridge, MA.

Schwarzlose, R.A. (1989) *The Formative Years, from Pretelegraph to 1865. The Rush to Institution, from 1865 to 1920*. Northwestern University Press, Evanston, IL.

Seely Brown, J. and Duguid, P. (2002) Local knowledge: innovation in the networked age. *Management Learning* 33(4), 427–437.

Shaaber, M. (1929) *Some Forerunners of the Newspaper in England, 1476–1622*. University of Pennsylvania Press, Philadelphia.

Shmanske, S. (1986) News as a public good: cooperative ownership, price commitments, and the success of the Associated Press. *Business History Review*, 60(1), 55–80.

Singer, J.B. (2005) The political j-blogger: "Normalizing" a new media form to fit old norms and practices. *Journalism*. 6(2), 173–198.

Slezkine, Y. (2004) *The Jewish Century*. Princeton University Press, Princeton, NJ.

Smith, A. (1978) The long road to objectivity and back again: the kinds of truth we get in journalism. In: Boyce, G., Curran, J., and Wingate, P. (eds) *Newspaper History: From the 17th Century to the Present Day*. Sage/Constable, London, 153–171.

144   *Bibliography*

Smith, A. (1979) *The Newspaper. An International History.* Thames and Hudson, London.

Smith, W.D. (1984) The function of commercial centers in the modernization of European capitalism: Amsterdam as an information exchange in the seventeenth century. *The Journal of Economic History* 44(4), 985–1005.

Soja, E.W. (1989) *Postmodern Geographies. The Reassertion of Space in Critical Social Theory.* Verso, London.

Spufford, P. (2002) *Power and Profit. The Merchant in Medieval Europe.* Thames and Hudson, London.

Sreberny-Mohammadi, A. with Nordenstreng, K., Stevenson, R., and Ugboajah, F. (1985) *Foreign News in the Media. International Reporting in 29 countries.* Reports and Papers on Mass Communication, No 93, United Nations Educational, Scientific, and Cultural Organization, Paris.

Standage, T. (1998) *The Victorian Internet: The Remarkable Story of the Telegraph and the Nineteenth Century's Online Pioneer.* Weidenfeld and Nicolson, London.

Stangerup, H. (1973/74) *Avisens historie*, Vols 1–3, Politikens Forlag and J.W. Cappelens Forlag, Copenhagen.

The State of the News Media 2008. An Annual Report on American Journalism. Available online at www.stateofthenewsmedia.org/2008/narrative_online_citizen_media.php?cat=6&media=5, accessed May 22, 2008.

Stephens, M. (1988) *A History of News.* Harcourt Brace College Publishers, Fort Worth, TX.

Stone, M. (1921) *Fifty Years a Journalist.* Doubleday, Page, and Co., New York.

Storey, G. (1951) *Reuters' Century 1851–1951.* Parrish, London.

Swindler, W.F. (1946) The AP anti-trust case in historical perspective. *Journalism Quarterly*, 23(4): 40–57.

Taylor, P.J. (2004) *World City Network. A Global Urban Analysis.* Routledge, London.

Thompson, J.B. (1994) Social theory and the media. In: Crowley, D. and Mitchell, D. (eds) *Communication Theory Today.* Polity Press, Cambridge, 27–43.

Thompson, J.B. (1995) *The Media and Modernity: A Social Theory of Media.* Polity Press, Cambridge.

Tomlinson, J. (1994) A phenomenology of globalisation? Giddens on global modernity. *European Journal of Communication* 9(2), 149–172.

Turkle, S. (1984) *The Second Self: Computers and the Human Spirit.* Simon and Schuster, New York.

UNESCO (1953) *News Agencies. Their Structure and Operation.* United Nations Educational, Scientific, and Cultural Organization, Paris.

UNESCO (1956) *The Problems of Transmitting Press Messages* United Nations Educational, Scientific, and Cultural Organization, Lausanne.

Van Couvering, E. (2008a) The history of the Internet search engine: navigational media and the traffic commodity. In Spink, A. and Zimmer, M. (eds) *Web Search: Interdisciplinary Perspectives*. Springer Verlag, Berlin, 177–206.

Van Couvering, E. (2008b) A personal interview on search engines. London, April 17.

Van der Wurff, R. (2005) Introduction: impacts of the Internet on newspapers in Europe. *Gazette*, 67(1): 5–7.

Vincent, D. (1989) *Literacy and Popular Culture: England 1750–1914*. Cambridge University Press, Cambridge.

Wallenstein, A. (2007) Yahoo news to tilt to a lilt. Available online at www.reuters.com/article/internetNews/idUSN2238102420070222, accessed May 22, 2008.

Waters, M. (1995) *Globalization*. Routledge, London.

Wilke, J. (1984) *Nachrichtenauswahl und Medienrealität in Vier Jahrhunderten*. Walter de Gruyter, Berlin.

Williams, F. (1953) *Transmitting World News*. United Nations Educational, Scientific, and Cultural Organization, Paris.

Winterbottom, W.A. (1929) Testimony before the Committee on Interstate Commerce. US Senate, 71st Congress, 2nd Session. In *Commission on Communications*. Government Printing Office, Washington, DC, 287–307.

Young, O.D. (1929) Testimony before the Committee on Interstate Commerce. US Senate, 71st Congress, 2nd Session. In *Commission on Communications*. Government Printing Office, Washington, DC, 20–47.

Zelizer, B. (1993) Journalists as interpretive communities, *Critical Studies in Mass Communication* 10(2): 219–37.

Index